Genre Pedagogy across the Curriculum

Genre Pedagogy across the Curriculum

Theory and Application in U.S. Classrooms and Contexts

Edited by
Luciana C. de Oliveira and Joshua Iddings

SHEFFIELD UK BRISTOL CT

Published by Equinox Publishing Ltd.

UK: Office 415, The Workstation, 15 Paternoster Row, Sheffield, South Yorkshire
S1 2BX

USA: ISD, 70 Enterprise Drive, Bristol, CT 06010

www.equinoxpub.com

First published 2014

British Library Cataloguing-in-Publication Data

A catalogue record for this book is available from the British Library.

ISBN 978 1 84553 241 3 (hardback)

Library of Congress Cataloging-in-Publication Data

Genre pedagogy across the curriculum : theory and application in U.S. classrooms and contexts / Edited by Luciana C. de Oliveira and Joshua Iddings.
pages cm
Includes bibliographical references and index.
ISBN 978-1-84553-241-3 (hb)
1. Language and languages--Study and teaching--United States. 2. Rhetoric--Study and teaching--United States. 3. Interdisciplinary approach in education--United States. 4. Critical pedagogy--United States. 5. Academic writing--Study and teaching--United States. 6. Functional linguistics--United States. 7. Structural linguistics--United States. I. De Oliveira, Luciana C., editor of compilation. II. Iddings, Joshua, editor of compilation.
P57.U7G43 2014
418.007'073--dc23

2014011968

Typeset by Steve Barganski
Printed and bound in Great Britain by Lightning Source

Dedication

To Mary Schleppegrell,
who has done so much to develop systemic functional linguistics in education
in the United States

Contents

List of contributors

Shireen Al-Adeimi is a doctoral student in Human Development and Education at the Harvard Graduate School of Education. Prior to pursuing her doctoral studies, she taught sixth grade Language Arts and Literature in New Mexico, and subsequently earned an MA in Teaching and Learning at the University of Michigan's School of Education. She is interested in language and literacy, with a focus on the written development of academic language and bilingual education research.

Deedra A. Arvin is a PhD student in Literacy and Language Education with a focus on English Language Learning in the Department of Curriculum and Instruction at Purdue University. Additionally, she works as a Test Development Program Manager at Data Recognition Corporation.

Benjamin Boche is a PhD student in the Literacy and Language Education program with a focus on English Education in the Department of Curriculum and Instruction at Purdue University. His research interests include teacher education, literacy, and technology.

María Estela Brisk is a Professor of Education at the Lynch School of Education, Boston College. Her research and teacher-training interests include elementary students' writing development, bilingual education, bilingual language and literacy acquisition, methods of teaching literacy, and preparation of mainstream teachers to work with bilingual learners. Dr. Brisk has served as a consultant in legal matters pertaining to bilingual education, and has worked closely with regional and local groups and school systems in developing their bilingual programs as well as mainstream programs that serve bilingual learners. Dr. Brisk is the author of five books and multiple articles and chapters.

Frank Daniello is an assistant professor in the College of Liberal Arts and Sciences at Lesley University. Daniello's educational work includes the use of systemic functional linguistics (SFL) to inform writing pedagogy, teacher leadership, and school reform. He holds a PhD from Boston College.

Luciana C. de Oliveira is Associate Professor of TESOL and Applied

Linguistics in the Department of Arts and Humanities at Teachers College, Columbia University. Dr. de Oliveira teaches TESOL methods courses to prepare teachers to work with English language learners (ELLs). Her research focuses on issues related to teaching ELLs at the K–12 level, including the role of language in learning the content areas; teacher education, advocacy and social justice; and nonnative English-speaking teachers in TESOL. Her work has appeared in *Teachers College Record, Journal of Teacher Education, Teaching Education, English Education, The History Teacher*, among other journals.

Marla De Rosa is doctoral candidate in the Curriculum and Instruction program at the Lynch School of Education, Boston College. She also teaches in the freshman writing program at Boston College and is Associate Director of the Writing Fellows program which supports the university's Writing across the Curriculum initiatives. Her research interests include working with bilingual, immigrant students in the areas of academic reading and writing.

Ruth Harman is an associate professor in the Language and Literacy Department at the University of Georgia. Her research focuses on how critical SFL-informed pedagogies, along with creative arts-based approaches, can be used to support the cultural and linguistic interests and needs of emergent bilingual and bidialectal students in K–12 contexts. At UGA she teaches systemic functional linguistics, critical discourse analysis, and second language literacy, and is involved in collaborative action research with local ESOL teachers and students.

Joshua G. Iddings is an assistant professor of English, Rhetoric, and Humanistic Studies at the Virginia Military Institute. His research interests include genre-based writing pedagogies, systemic functional linguistics, teaching for social justice, and Appalachian studies. He currently teaches courses in cultural rhetoric, language and style, and first year composition.

Marshall Klassen is a PhD student in Literacy and Language Education in the Department of Curriculum and Instruction at Purdue University. His research interests are second language acquisition, diversifying instruction for English language learners (ELLs) in a K–12 setting, and teacher education for ELLs. He is currently researching diversifying instruction for ELLs in a kindergarten classroom with a focus on mathematics discourse.

Shu-Wen Lan completed her PhD in Literacy and Language Education in the Department of Curriculum and Instruction at Purdue University. Her research focuses on the teaching and learning of English language learners (ELLs) in elementary science classrooms. She has taught undergraduate courses to prepare pre-service teachers to work with ELLs in elementary content-area classrooms.

Dominique Lowery Franklin is a PhD student specializing in Literacy and Language Education in the Department of Curriculum and Instruction at Purdue University in West Lafayette, Indiana. She has served as a Spanish teacher and high school assistant principal in Atlanta, Georgia, the Director of Federal Programs for the Community Schools of Frankfort in Frankfort, Indiana, and currently serves as the high school principal at Hoosier Academy in Indianapolis, Indiana. Her research interests include the influence of English language learners' (ELLs) involvement in extracurricular activities on ELLs' academic achievement, ELL policies for school administration, and equity and access for ELLs.

Michael Maune is a PhD student in Literacy and Language Education at Purdue University. He has taught for five years at various levels including middle school, high school, and college. His research focuses on educational linguistics and genre pedagogy from a systemic functional linguistics perspective.

Jason Moore is a postdoctoral research fellow at the University of Michigan's School of Education and a former high school English teacher. He earned an MA from the University of Virginia. His research explores ways in which a functional approach to language can support English language learners' disciplinary reading and writing in the English Language Arts.

Catherine L. O'Hallaron is a postdoctoral research fellow at the University of Michigan's School of Education, where she earned her PhD in Literacy, Language, and Culture. Her research interests include linguistic approaches to studying English learners' writing development and the use of functional linguistic pedagogy in enhancing teachers' writing instruction.

Annemarie Sullivan Palincsar is the Jean and Charles Walgreen Jr. Chair of Reading and Literacy, Arthur F. Thurnau Professor, and a teacher educator in Educational Studies at the University of Michigan. Her research focuses on the design of learning environments that support self-regulation in learning activity, especially for children who experience difficulty learning in school. Her book, co-authored with Linda Kucan, *Comprehension Instruction through Text-based Discussion*, was published in 2013.

J. Andrés Ramírez is an assistant professor in the Curriculum, Culture, and Educational Inquiry Department at Florida Atlantic University. He teaches courses in TESOL, Bilingual Education and Applied Linguistics. His scholarly work explores the linguistic, cultural, and economic conditions constraining and enabling the academic literacy achievement of culturally and linguistically diverse students in the United States. He anchors his academic work on poststructural materialism, critical discourse studies. His current scholarship focuses on the intersection between bilingual language development theory and practice and Systemic Functional Linguistics (SFL).

Amber M. Simmons received her PhD in Language and Literacy Education from the University of Georgia and currently works in the Gwinnett County School District in Georgia. Her previous work, published in *English Journal*, *Journal of Adolescent and Adult Literacy*, and *SIGNAL Journal*, focused on using adolescent and traditional texts in the classroom to support critical literacy. Amber's more recent work centers on implementing critical systemic functional linguistics and discourse analysis methods in the classroom as a way to encourage an ELA curriculum that focuses on language as a social process.

Mary J. Schleppegrell is professor of education and chair of Educational Studies at the University of Michigan's School of Education. Her research studies the role of language in learning with particular attention to the needs of English language learners, and she draws on systemic functional linguistics to identify the demands of teaching and learning in different subject areas. She is the author of *The Language of Schooling* (Erlbaum, 2004) as well as other books, journal articles, and book chapters. She is currently involved in a three-year project to develop a functional grammar approach for elementary school teachers and English language learners.

Carrie Symons is a doctoral student in Literacy, Language, and Culture at the University of Michigan's School of Education. She earned an MA in Curriculum and Instruction from the University of Colorado, Boulder. Prior to pursuing her doctorate, Carrie was an elementary classroom teacher for ten years. With a focus on literacy and language development in the elementary grades, she is currently a research assistant on the *Language and Meaning* project directed by Mary Schleppegrell and Annemarie Palincsar.

Foreword

By the 1980s, successive waves of migration following WWII had transformed Australia. A predominantly "Anglo/Irish" nation, protected by its "White Australia" policy, had become a celebrated multicultural society—one in which even its Indigenous people were beginning to have a public voice. School populations of course reflected this change, and educators began to take responsibility for respecting the diversity of their diverse student cohorts at the same time as facilitating their paths through school. Alongside this demographic shift "progressive" approaches to education began to replace tradition ones, especially in infants and primary school. As far as writing instruction was concerned, process writing was adopted across states, inspired by the work of its founding guru, Donald Graves. Students were encouraged to select their own topics for writing, and work their way through the stages of the process writing curriculum genre—drafting, conferencing, publishing, and the like. Teachers backed off, playing a facilitating role (as guides on the side), encouraging students to choose their own topics and write in any form they choose. And then teachers and parents began to notice, especially in schools with large numbers of working-class, migrant or Indigenous children: "This doesn't seem to work for my kids."

It was in this cultural context that "Sydney School" approaches to reading and writing took hold. Functional linguists in and around the University of Sydney began to work with educators concerned about the state of literacy education in Australian schools. In primary school, for example, they observed the adverse effects of process writing as far as the range of writing undertaken by students was concerned and the lack of any meaningful language development. Texts got longer as the students got older, but they kept writing, understandably, in the genres they were already familiar with from their oral culture—observation comments and recounts, using spoken language to do so. They were not engaging in writing relevant to the themes of their science, social science, and English curricula; they were not doing the kinds of writing they would be expected to produce across subjects in secondary school; and they were not dealing with texts they might encounter outside of school, when some of them might in fact be negotiating with businesses, health providers, and government agencies as the most fluent and literate English speaker in their family. Genre-based literacy programs were developed, as an issue of social justice, to address challenges of this kind.

Given the stranglehold of formal paradigms as far as language science in America is concerned, I never thought I would live to see the day when literacy programs informed by functional linguistics began to be explored in the U.S.A. But I was wrong. Because there, a couple of decades after it happened in Australia, teachers and parents, especially in schools with large numbers of working-class, migrant, African American, Latino, or Indigenous children came to the same realization: "Schools don't seem to be working for my kids." This collection of papers reflects this frustration and showcases the response of concerned educators who took it upon themselves to adapt "Sydney School" initiatives for students in American classrooms.

What a thrill it has been over the past few years to be able to engage in the refreshing dialogue that the work of these teacher/linguists has introduced into the development of genre-based literacy programs around the world. The editors, de Oliveira and Iddings, have here brought together papers from a range of courageous and innovative educators who are determined to make significant changes to the allocation of literacy resources in U.S. schools. Their achievements and progress, and their modesty in the face of the work that remains to be done, are inspirational. My heartfelt thanks to all the contributors for making our Australian initiatives feel all the more worthwhile. And a special note of thanks to the most modest of these contributors, Mary Schleppegrell, for catalyzing so much of the work that thrives herein.

J. R. Martin

1 Genre pedagogy across the curriculum in U.S. classrooms and contexts

Luciana C. de Oliveira and Joshua G. Iddings

The systemic functional linguistics (SFL) genre approach utilized in this volume is rooted in work developed in Australia since the 1980s, and adapted for use in different classrooms and contexts across the United States. Known in the U.S.A. as the Sydney School, this view of genre connects grammatical knowledge to the achievement of social purposes. In SFL terms, genres are "recurrent configurations of meanings … that … enact the social practices of a given culture," or "staged, goal oriented social processes. Staged, because it usually takes us more than one step to reach our goals; goal oriented because we feel frustrated if we don't accomplish the final steps …; social because writers shape their texts for readers of particular kinds" (Martin & Rose, 2008, p. 6). Different stages within a particular genre are identifiable by their linguistic and grammatical patterns to achieve a social purpose in a particular context. A genre-based approach has much potential for application in classrooms as it helps students see how different language features build genre stages and learn how to structure the kinds of texts they are expected to write in school. This potential is what has been recognized by scholars in the U.S.A. over the past several years. This volume compiles much of the work by U.S. scholars who have applied this genre-based approach in classrooms, within teacher education programs, and other contexts.

This collection aims to describe both theoretical and practical applications of a genre-based approach from the elementary through university levels. While SFL genre-based curricula have been proposed for many years throughout countries such as Australia and others, much less is known about how this curriculum is being utilized in the United States, a country with a much richer history in such disciplines as Rhetoric and Composition as well as Chomskyan formal linguistics that affect our knowledge of language and education. This is the first edited volume of its kind focusing on research conducted in the United States. This volume aims to highlight ways in which the SFL genre-based pedagogy is being theorized and applied in this relatively new context.

While there are other genre-based pedagogies in the U.S.A., SFL-based genre pedagogies illuminate the importance of language and linguistic choice within the curriculum, aiming to make these choices explicitly understood in the mind of scholars, teachers, and students alike. By highlighting the importance of an explicit, accessible curriculum through language awareness of commonly used pedagogical texts, each chapter shows how this pedagogy can be adapted and utilized across many different disciplines and student age groups.

Key concepts in SFL genre theory

The genre-based approach utilized in this volume is rooted in an SFL theoretical description of language:

> A text is the product of ongoing selection in a very large network of systems—a system network. Systemic theory gets its name from the fact that the grammar of a language is represented in the form of system networks, not as an inventory of structures. Of course, structure is an essential part of the description; but it is interpreted as the outward form taken by systemic choices, not as the defining characteristic of language. A language is a resource for making meaning, and meaning resides in systemic patterns of choice. (Halliday & Matthiessen, 2004, p. 23)

Since texts are instances of the systemic choices being made, we can work backwards from the text to discover the meaning choices which have been made by writers and what function they might serve. In addition, we can discover here what meaning choices have been made over other possible choices. Although each chapter in this volume utilizes SFL genre theory in different ways, each does so with these key concepts underlying their work.

There are several other important theoretical aspects of SFL which an analyst can consider. One is the genre, or the realization of the context of culture, represented by the culturally expected structure of types of texts and the ways in which register variables are realized (Eggins, 2004; Martin & Rose, 2007, 2008). Register, or the realization of the context of situation, is represented by choices of field, mode, and tenor (Eggins, 2004; Halliday & Matthiessen, 2004). The field concerns what the "language is being used to talk about." The mode concerns "the role language plays in the interaction," whether it is written or spoken. Finally, the tenor concerns the "role relationships [play] between the interactants" (Eggins, 2004, p. 90). These three variables determine what Halliday calls the three metafunctions in language (Halliday & Matthiessen, 2004).

The three metafunctions in an SFL view of language are the interpersonal, textual, and ideational. These three metafunctions characterize the "resources of the lexico-grammar of every language" (Halliday & Matthiessen, 2004, p. 29). In other words, these three kinds of meanings are realized as instances in the lexico-grammatical patterns which we see in a text. Thus, the analyst not only looks at the contextual factors behind a composition—genre and register in Martin and Rose's (2007, 2008) terms—but they also should understand the language features which realize the specific registers and genres under consideration (viewing language from the roles they play across and within metafunctions).

The three metafunctions can be briefly characterized as follows. The interpersonal metafunction refers to how a clause is represented as an exchange between speaker and listener, or reader and writer (Eggins, 2004; Halliday & Matthiessen, 2004), and is connected to the tenor of the text. Lexico-grammatically, one aspect that we analyze is related to the presence or absence of the subject and finite elements of the clauses and in what order they occur with respect to one another (Eggins, 2004; Halliday & Matthiessen, 2004). These are important because they realize the grammatical choice of the mood of a clause: either declarative, interrogative, or imperative. Next, the textual metafunction realizes how the clause is expressed as a message (Eggins, 2004; Halliday & Matthiessen, 2004) and is connected to the mode of the text. Lexico-grammatically, we analyze the text related to the ways in which the Themes and Rhemes are instantiated in each clause. The Theme is the first experiential element of the clause and the Rheme encompasses the remaining bit of the clause (Halliday & Matthiessen, 2004). Additionally, it is useful to track the thematic development through texts which, in part, helps organize the overall text as it moves from stage to stage and within the stage. We also can discuss hyper-Themes and macro-Themes, where hyper-Themes serve as organizers of paragraphs, typically called topic sentences (Martin & Rose, 2007, p. 195), and macro-Themes are referred to as "higher level Themes" that "predict hyperThemes" (p. 197). Movements within stages are also called phases (Martin & Rose, 2008).

Finally, the ideational metafunction realizes the ways in which the clause represents the experiences an author/speaker expresses (Eggins, 2004; Halliday & Matthiessen, 2004) and is connected to the field of the text. Lexico-grammatically speaking, we are concerned here with the Participants (typically expressed through nouns) engaged in some kinds of Processes (typically expressed through verbs) under certain Circumstances (typically expressed through prepositional/adverbial phrases) (Eggins, 2004; Halliday & Matthiessen, 2004).

The relationships between genre, register, and language can be visually represented via a figure such as the one adapted here from Martin and Rose (2008, p. 17) and presented below as Figure 1.1. This figure presents a series of three co-tangential circles, with genre as the largest circle, register (field, mode, and tenor) as the next largest, and the three metafunction variables as

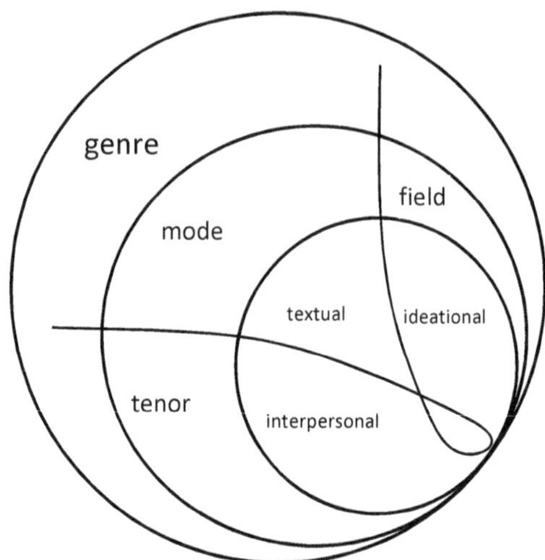

Figure 1.1. The SFL Genre Strata Model (Martin & Rose, 2008, p. 17)

the smallest circle. What this represents is that genre is realized by choices in the register variables: tenor, mode, and field. In turn, register is realized as choices among the three metafunction variables: interpersonal, textual, and ideational. The criss-crossed line in the middle of the figure represents the interrelationship among each of these different levels of linguistic analysis and the metaredundancy (Martin & Rose, 2007, p. 308) across each of the levels. Again, for example, the interpersonal language choices are realizations of the tenor which the writer/speaker is expressing which is also a realization of the genre in which the writer/speaker is constructing their text.

Overview of chapters

This section provides an overview of each chapter in the volume. In keeping with the SFL custom of using an initial capital letter for all functional labels such as Theme, each chapter uses capital letters for all functional terms.

In Chapter 2, "Young Writers' Attempts at Making Meaning through Complex Sentence Structures while Writing a Variety of Genres," María Estela Brisk and Marla De Rosa focus on the formation of clause complexes, i.e. combinations of more than one clause, and the logico-semantic relations between the clauses in these complexes as one aspect of the written language that changes as students progress in their ability to write. They report on a study that analyzed students' texts to understand how children use language resources to create logico-semantic relations when constructing clause complexes and provide a description of children's developmental patterns as they learn to construct clause-complexes. They then provide an analysis of the types of clause-complexes that children in grades 4–8 create in uncoached Personal Recounts and those they create when they receive instruction in other genres. The results suggest the value of instruction in other genres as it calls on children to construct a wider range of clause-complexes.

In Chapter 3, "Tackling a Genre: Situating SFL Genre Pedagogy in a New Context," Mary J. Schleppegrell, Jason Moore, Shireen Al-Adeimi, Catherine L. O'Hallaron, Annemarie Sullivan Palincsar, and Carrie Symons focus on a project where the authors designed materials to support the literacy development of English language learners (ELLs) through functional grammar. They report on how they developed and supported the writing of a genre they called a Recount and identify issues that emerged in classroom interaction and students' written products. They show how the SFL genre approach offers a flexible framework for presenting new genres in ways that are relevant to particular contexts and settings.

In Chapter 4, "Elementary Grade Teachers using Systemic Functional Linguistics to Inform Genre-based Writing Instruction," Frank Daniello focuses on changes to fourth and fifth grade teachers' writing instruction over three years in an urban elementary school. Daniello describes an SFL-based school–university partnership that provided teachers ongoing professional development focused on fostering teachers' understanding of SFL theory and the taught genres: Recount, Procedure, Narrative, Report, Explanation, and Exposition. He describes how teachers' lessons evolved regarding the teaching of genre and how their writing instruction with students became more precise. He identifies changes in instruction, demonstrating how teachers operationalized SFL theory in practice to educate students about genre.

In Chapter 5, "Genre-based Principles in a Content-Based English as a Second Language Pull-out Classroom," J. Andrés Ramírez describes the genre-based procedures and pedagogical principles that enriched ELL students' academic literacy ontogenesis as this approach prevented them from entirely missing the science content they were not getting at the time of ESL pull-out instruction. He shows how meeting ELLs varied educational needs can be a great opportunity for core content teachers as well as for ESL teachers and demonstrates how systemic functional linguistics and its associated genre-based methodology can be used successfully so that ESL students with developmental needs in English can also attain high levels of academic literacy, even when pull-out is the prevalent way students receive ESL services.

In Chapter 6, "Critical Systemic Functional Linguistics and the Teaching of Literary Narratives in Secondary School English," Ruth Harman and Amber

M. Simmons describe a critical language approach applied in a secondary English classroom. Harman and Simmons discuss how this approach was developed over time in an Advanced Placement (AP) Language and Composition course and illustrate how the culturally diverse group of students learned to analyze Rowling's (1997) fiction using the SFL interpersonal register metafunction. They conclude by discussing the importance of using critical SFL approaches in K–12 and in teacher education classrooms.

In Chapter 7, "A Genre-based Approach to Teaching the Book Review," Benjamin Boche focuses on what types of information textbooks provide to both teachers and students in regards to writing a commonplace school genre: the Book Review. He analyzes a sample book review in a textbook using a systematic functional linguistics approach highlighting important findings. By using both the textbook directions and the SFL analysis, a more well-rounded and informed approach to teaching book reviews can help teachers and students master this important genre.

Chapter 8, "Filling in the Gaps: Genre as a Scaffold to the Text Types of the Common Core State Standards," presents genre analyses of sample writings featured in Appendix C of the widely-adopted K–12 Common Core State Standards (CCSS). Michael Maune and Marshall Klassen examine how student writing samples fulfill the genre expectations detailed by genre research in SFL. They closely examine the samples and annotations in the CCSS and then provide an SFL analysis of those same texts. They conclude with a proposal of how these two frameworks may be used together to create a more coherent whole that will be beneficial to both educators and students alike.

In Chapter 9, "Standardized Assessments for English Language Learners: Implications of Differing Expectations," Deedra A. Arvin and Dominique Lowery analyze and compare two informational passages used in high-stakes testing in Indiana for high school students. They focus on the textual metafunction by analyzing both thematic development and cohesion for both texts and further identify potential challenges for ELLs. This chapter describes differences between the sample passages for the two assessments and discusses implications of these differences.

In Chapter 10, "Writing a Dissertation Proposal: Genre Expectations," Joshua Iddings, Shu-Wen Lan, and Luciana C. de Oliveira analyze the genre expectations of the dissertation proposal genre, one of the key genres in a PhD program in the United States. They specifically focus on some concrete language features of effective dissertation proposals, which both advisors and students can utilize when teaching and learning to write their own proposals. Through an explicit discussion of their own dissertation proposals, the authors highlight those language features which best realize the dissertation proposal genre in qualitative educational research.

While each chapter throughout this volume utilizes different aspects of Sydney School genre theory for educational purposes, one of the key underlying assumptions in each is the centrality of a language-based pedagogy to school curricula. In fact, it is our hope that readers will see the importance of these approaches for students and practitioners at all levels of schooling, whether primary, secondary, or tertiary, and no matter the linguistic background of the students in each classroom.

References

Eggins, S. (2004). *An introduction to systemic functional linguistics* (2nd ed.). New York: Continuum.

Halliday, M. A. K., & Matthiessen, C. M. I. M. (2004). *An introduction to functional grammar* (3rd ed.). London: Arnold.

Martin, J. R., & Rose, D. (2007). *Working with discourse: Meaning beyond the clause* (2nd ed.). London: Continuum.

Martin, J. R., & Rose, D. (2008). *Genre relations: Mapping culture*. London: Equinox.

Rowling, J. K. (1997). *Harry Potter and the sorcerer's stone*. London: Bloombury.

2 Young writers' attempts at making meaning through complex sentence structures while writing a variety of genres

María Estela Brisk and Marla De Rosa

Writing across genres is a crucial skill in a 21st-century academic and workforce landscape that increasingly requires linguistic flexibility and mastery (National Commission on Writing, 2003, 2005). The need to develop successful writers is paramount. It has thus been recommended that writing assume a prominent role in school curricula, and that teachers provide more writing instruction to students (National Commission on Writing, 2003).

Most children develop written language out of their experience with the spoken language, but oral and written language play different roles in our society and have features that distinguish these modes. As Halliday (1989) points out, "writing and speaking are not just alternative ways of doing the same things; rather, they are ways of doing different things" (p. xv). The initial demands of writing are such that children are usually behind compared to their oral language development (Christie, 2012; Loban, 1976). Studies comparing the spoken and written language of elementary age children show changes between third and sixth grades that indicate these are important years for supporting written language development (Kroll & Lempers, 1981; Lull, 1929). Christie (2012) suggests that children's language in their late childhood/early adolescent stage (ages 9–13) begins "to change, facilitated by a gradual expansion of language resources, so that children can make meanings in new ways" (p. 28). These changes pave the way for the grammar of written language.

As children transition from oral to written discourse, they achieve a growing control of the thematic patterns of their writing and show more control of internal reference to build cohesion in their texts. Students learn to compress more information into different types of prepositional phrases and to use nominalizations and other strategies to expand noun groups and create denser texts (Hunt, 1965). This is the phase in which students also demonstrate an increased ability to create different clause types and clause interdependencies (Christie, 2012).

The formation of clause-complexes, i.e. combinations of more than one clause and the logico-semantic relations between the clauses in these complexes, is one aspect of the written language that changes as students progress in their ability to write. Different genres call on students to construct particular types of clause-complexes in their writing. The purpose of this study is to analyze students' texts to understand how children in grades 4–8 use language resources to construct clause-complexes in different genres and disciplines.

In this chapter we provide a description of the clause-complex and children's developmental patterns as they learn to construct clause-complexes. We then provide an analysis of the types of clause-complexes that children in grades 4–8 create in uncoached Personal Recounts and those they create when they receive instruction in other genres. The results suggest the value of instruction in other genres as it calls on children to construct a wider range of clause-complexes.

The clause-complex

The central source for making meaning is the clause (Halliday & Matthiessen, 2004; Thompson, 2004). Two or more clauses can be combined to produce a larger unit, called a clause-complex and different genres call for different types of clause-complexes. These clauses "are linked to one another by means of some kind of logico-semantic relation" (Halliday & Matthiessen, 2004, p. 363). The interdependence among clauses is usually signaled by conjunctions (Eggins, 2004; Thompson, 2004). Clauses in a clause-complex relate on two dimensions, one is the type of dependency, or taxis, and the other is the logico-semantic relation between the clauses (see Table 2.1). The logical metafunction manages the connection of the meanings expressed by the clauses (Thompson, 2004). Taxis manages the dependence or independence of the clauses within the clause-complex. There are two types of dependency: parataxis and hypotaxis. Parataxis is one of equality, commonly known as coordination. In hypotaxis, or subordination, one of the clauses is dominant and the other dependent. Embedded clauses do not form clause-complexes since they function as a constituent of the clause. The relation is within the clause (Halliday & Matthiessen, 2004).

There is a wide range of possible logico-semantic relations between clauses. The two basic types of relationships are projection and expansion (Halliday & Matthiessen, 2004). In projection, one clause indicates what someone said (locution) or thought (idea). The other clause expresses what was actually said or thought, either quoted or paraphrased (Eggins, 2004).

There are three ways of expanding a clause: elaboration, extension, and enhancement. In this type of clause-complex, the secondary clause expands what is expressed in the primary clause. There are many different possibilities to build on the meaning, often signaled by a conjunction or other connective (for details see Table 2.1). Thus, when combining clauses, writers need to decide the meaning to be expressed, the connective that will signal the type of expansion, and the order in which they will place the clauses.

Different genres call on writers to construct particular types of clause-complexes in their writing. In time-structured genres such as Narratives and Personal Recounts, the text connectives are used to create temporal relationships between clauses. In genres that are organized around ideas, such as Expositions, the text connectives are more likely to do with reasoning and serve to sequence ideas, add information, and clarify. In Explanations, the connectives are needed to convey the logical reasoning or causal relationships (Derewianka & Jones, 2012).

Table 2.1. The clause-complex: taxis and logico-semantic relations

<table>
<tr><td colspan="2" rowspan="2">Taxis
(type of interdependency)</td><td colspan="2">Parataxis (coordination)</td></tr>
<tr><td colspan="2">Hypotaxis (subordination)</td></tr>
<tr><td colspan="4"></td></tr>
<tr><td rowspan="3">Logico-semantic relation</td><td rowspan="2">Projection</td><td>Locution
(verbal processes)</td><td rowspan="2">Quotes are paratactic.
Reports are hypotactic: She said that she was not coming.
Embedding: see Thompson, 2004, p. 212</td></tr>
<tr><td>Idea
(mental processes)</td></tr>
<tr><td>Expansion</td><td>Elaboration
(does not introduce a new element of meaning)</td><td>Exposition (in other words): The secondary clause restates the core meaning of the primary clause in different words, different point of view, or reinforces the message.
Exemplification: Develops the meaning by becoming more specific or citing an example for example, for instance, in particular.
Clarification (to be precise): Clarifies with an Explanation or explanatory comment, in fact, actually, indeed, at least, what I mean is.</td></tr>
</table>

Logico-semantic relation (*cont.*)	Expansion (*cont.*)	Extension (one clause extends the meaning of the other by adding something new)		**Addition**: [paratactic] simply additive (*and*), negative addition (*nor*) or adversative (*but*) [hypotactic] *whereas, while.* **Variation**: One clause is in partial or total replacement of the other (*or, instead of, except for*). [hypotactic, non-finite] *besides, apart from, instead of, other than, without.*
			Temporal	When? At what time? *Then, next, afterwards, just then, at the same time, before that, soon, after a while, meanwhile, all the time, until then, up to that point, now.*
			Spatial	Where? Whereabouts? Extent: as far as Point: where Spread: Wherever, everywhere
			Manner	How? In what way? By what means? Like what? [means: *and + in that way; thus*] [comparison: *and + similarly, so, thus*]
			Comparative	*Likewise, similarly, in a different way*
			Causal • reason • purpose • result	**Reason**: *because, as, since, in case, seeing that, considering, so, then, therefore, consequently, hence, because of that, for, in consequence, as a result, on account of this, for that reason, for that purpose, with this in view* **Purpose**: *in order to, so as to, for (the sake of), with the aim of, for fear of* Result: *so that* (finite), *to* (non-finite)
			Conditional	**Positive**: *if, in the event, provided that, as long as* **Negative**: *unless, but for, without*
			Concessive	*But, yet, still, though, despite, despite this, however, even so, all the same, nevertheless, even if, even though, although, in spite of, without*

Sources: Eggins, 2004; Halliday & Matthiessen, 2004; Thompson, 2004.

Development of the clause-complex

Research on the development of the clause-complex has been carried out more frequently with respect to oral language development. The development in written language seems to follow similar patterns but usually lags one to two years behind oral development (Loban, 1976).

Development in oral language

As their oral language develops, children follow a predictable pattern in their use of connectives that join clauses. Katz and Brent (1968) examined the use of connectives in first and fifth graders with college sophomores as a control group. They tested students' use of connectives and children's ability to explain the use of connectives. They found the following sequence of the acquisition of relations and connectives: additive, temporal, causal, and adversative. Not only did temporal connections appear before causal, but they were used to express causal connections. For example, *It started to rain, then we ran into the house*, instead of *We ran into the house because it started to rain.* This need for mirroring the temporal order of events started to decrease by age 12. Adversative connectives and relations were the most difficult for the students. Most first graders and one third of the fifth graders selected the incorrect usage of the connectives *but* and *although.* Naturalistic studies of English language acquisition and production that followed Katz and Brent's experimental study found similar patterns (Bloom et al., 1980; Eisenberg, 1980; Spooren & Sanders, 2008). Bloom et al. (1980) also found that the acquisition order of specific connectives was as follows: *and, and then, because, so, but*. Of these connectives, *and* is first used for additive relations, and later also for temporal, causal and adversative relations.

While these studies tell us a lot about the development of connectives in oral language, the above research does not examine whether the patterns extend to written-language development. One of the few studies to link development in oral language to development in written language is Loban's (1976) longitudinal study of 211 students from kindergarten through twelfth grade. One purpose of the study was to discern developmental patterns in both oral and written language. Loban found that, compared to oral language development, writing development was more erratic, and large upward trends are followed by consolidation of growth and often downward shifts. However, most students made notable advances in writing development in fifth, eighth, tenth, and twelfth grade, and these advances occurred one to two years after similar advances in oral language. This link between oral and written language development allows some inferences to be drawn from the research on oral language development. It seems reasonable to assume the order of development of connectives would also apply to their development in written language.

Development in written language

Researchers have also examined the developmental patterns in children's ability to construct written clause-complexes. Hunt (1965) analyzed the taxis or subordination patterns in the writing of students in fourth, eighth, and twelfth grade. He found that, even in fourth grade, students will subordinate some clauses to each other, but not as many as twelfth graders. Fourth graders will embed some coordinated clauses inside a single clause and create some complex nominal groups. Hunt concluded that the average fourth grade child can produce all possible grammatical structures. The difference is that fourth graders do not produce as many structures at the same time as older students, and twelfth graders are able to convey the same meaning with far fewer words than younger writers.

Studies on the emergence of logico-semantic relations in children's written language focus mostly on additive extension and enhancement relations. Initially, connected clauses follow a temporal organization following the order of things in the world (Kress, 1982). The default connective used is *and* even when the logico-semantic relation may not be additive, but could be temporal or causal. Temporal enhancement relations appear first, followed by reason, condition, place, purpose, manner, and concession (Christie, 2010; Kress, 1982; Loban, 1976; Perera, 1984). In early childhood, written clauses are often singular or joined by additive connectives. Temporal clauses are usually the first dependent clauses to be used, and they are often in a marked Theme position in the sentence. When children are 9 to 12, clauses of reason, condition and purpose begin to appear in their writing. Towards the end of this stage, children begin to use non-finite clauses and clauses of concession and some clauses of projection (Christie, 2010, 2012; Christie & Derewianka, 2008). Christie (2012) notes that during this stage, clauses are organized more carefully with more clause interdependencies. Children's dependent clauses of enhancement are mainly of time and reason; however, conditional clauses can occur.

Context of the study

This study took place in a small urban Catholic school in the state of Massachusetts with approximately 250 students in pre-kindergarten through eighth grade. Seventy-seven percent of the students speak a language other than English at home with the majority being Spanish (49.7%) and Vietnamese (20.2%). There are also a variety of other languages represented such as Haitian Creole, Portuguese, Gujarati, Arabic, and Amharic.

This school has been working for the past year in partnership with the principal author of this paper and two of her doctoral students with a focus on introducing teachers to a writing approach informed by systemic functional linguistics (SFL). All teachers received a one-day institute in the summer before school started where the approach was introduced. Monthly professional development continued with teachers in grades 4 through 8. Topics of the professional development sessions included the general framework of SFL theory, including context of culture, register, various genres, and specific language features of different genres. These sessions reinforced the genres the teachers were in the process of teaching and the teaching and learning cycle. In addition to presentation of the theory, teachers discussed mentor texts and student writing. Teachers were observed and supported with the implementation. Neither the professional development nor classroom instruction explicitly taught clause-complex formation or logico-semantic relations.

Methodology

The study focused on the writing products of students in grades 4–8. Two types of student work were collected: on the spot, or uncoached writing in response to a prompt requiring a Personal Recount and writing within units of instruction in a variety of genres depending on the subject matter and teacher preference. With the exception of the uncoached Personal Recount, students received instruction in each of the genre types. Students wrote Personal Recounts and Autobiographies in English Language Arts classes; Parables in Religion classes; Procedures, Personal Recounts, Reports, and Explanations in Science, and Exposition in Social Studies. For the purpose of this study, the writing of three or four students per grade level for each genre implemented was chosen for detailed analysis with respect to dependency and logico-semantic relations. A total of 83 pieces of writing produced by 19 students were examined. The 19 students spoke a variety of languages other than English at home, but for each grade level there was writing from a Spanish and a Vietnamese bilingual student since those were the dominant languages spoken by students.

To analyze the data, the writing was sorted by grade level and genre. All the verbal groups functioning as a Process in each text were underlined. Then the text was divided into clauses and clause-complexes. Within the clause-complexes the components were separated, using notations found in the literature where ||| separates clauses and || separates the components of a compound clause-complex and | separates clauses within a subordinate clause-complex (Butt et al., 2000; Thompson, 2004). The clause-complexes were first analyzed with regard to the logico-semantic relations and then reanalyzed with respect to dependency once it became clear how interconnected the two dimensions were. The clause-complexes were classified according to the type of dependency and logico-semantic relations included in Table 2.1. The logico-semantic relations that appeared in the uncoached Personal Recount were identified first, then the writing in different genres that emerged during content area lessons were reviewed for the same types of relations or any additional ones. A table was constructed with examples of each type of logico-semantic relations for each grade in which they appeared, distinguishing between parataxis and hypotaxis. The code for the student—first name/last name initials, grade level, genre, and date—was indicated, for example KI, 5th, Parables, 10/24/11. Instances of problematic relationships were also inserted in the table. The two authors reviewed all the data to check on accuracy of classification and discussed complex problems.

Results

Students made numerous attempts at using clause-complexes in their writing. The types of relations varied in relation to the particular genres the students were encouraged to write. Performance differed depending on the grade level and genre. Finally, students were more likely to write paratactic clauses rather than hypotactic clauses. The conjunction *and* was the default choice, especially when students wrote their uncoached Personal Recounts (UPRs).

Logico-semantic relations and genres

There was a noticeable difference in the use of these relationships between the writing of UPRs and that of all the other genres done as part of writing instruction. Instruction supported the use of more relationships in more genres and at an earlier grade level. Table 2.2 shows the relations that appeared in the UPRs (indicated with a ✓). In addition to these same relations, writing in the instructed genres showed a number of other relations (indicated by naming the genre). The only relation that was used in UPRs and not in instructed genres was spatial.

Table 2.2. The clause-complex: types of logico-semantic relations

Types of logico-semantic relations			**Grade level use**				
			4	5	6	7	8
Projection	Locution (verbal processes)			✓	✓	✓	✓
	Idea (mental processes)			✓	✓	✓	✓
Expansion	Elaboration	Exposition					
		Exemplifi-cation					
		Clarification:				Exposition	
	Extension	Addition • additive	✓	✓	✓	✓	✓
		• negative addition					
		• adversative	Report Explanation	Parables Autobiographies			
		Variation		Exposition	✓		
	Enhancement	Temporal	✓	✓	Science Procedure	✓	✓
		Spatial		✓		✓	
		Manner					
		Comparative					ELA Personal Narr.
		Causal • reason	Personal Recount (Science) Report	✓	✓	✓	✓
		• purpose			Science Procedure		
		Conditional • positive	Explanation		Science Procedure		ELA Personal Narr.
		• negative					
		Concessive	Report Procedural Recount		Science Procedure		✓

Uncoached Personal Recounts

When writing in this genre students expressed all forms of projections, both locution and idea beginning in fifth grade. Locutions were mostly in the form of report or indirect speech (hypotactic), *They even told me || that it was a two hour RIDE!!* (WF, 5th, Personal Recount writing prompt, 9/19/11) With respect to expansion, additive extensions and temporal enhancement first appeared in fourth grade. Causal enhancement appeared from fifth grade on. Occasional uses of other relationships were adversative and variation in sixth grade, spatial in fifth and seventh grades, and concessive in eighth grade.

The most noticeable features of the UPRs were the use of temporal order and connection with the conjunction *and*, whether it was an additive relation or any other. The example below is from a fourth grader. However, similar writing occurred in UPRs through eighth grade.

> My story is about the first time I went to Water Country. My Uncle picked up my Aunt and I. Then, we went to pick up my cousion Tommy and a few friends. We sat in the car for a couple of hours. Finally, we made it. We changed into our 5 bathing suits <u>and</u> found a place to sit. **[temporal]** The first ride we went on was a huge water slide. I got a floaty <u>and</u> made my way up the stairs, **[temporal]** They, I slid down <u>and</u> laughed the whole way. **[additive]** Next, I went to the wave pool, it was so much fun. The waves pulled us up and down. We took pictures <u>and</u> swam around. **[temporal]** The we went to a place that looked like a river. We all got a floaty <u>and</u> sat on it. The water pulled us the whole way, <u>and</u> water splashed everywhere **[additive]**. We went around the river a few times <u>and</u> got out **[temporal]**. Then we had lunch. We ate hot dogs, French fries, chips, and ice cream. Then my Aunt and I went on another water slide. We got a floaty that could hold two people, <u>and</u> waited in line **[temporal]**. We sat down <u>and</u> screamed the whole way **[additive]**. It was so much fun. Then we went into a round pool <u>and</u> the water pushed us around and around **[temporal]**. We went in the wave pool again <u>and</u> my Ant rented a floaty **[causal]**. She pulled me around <u>and</u> I relaxed **[causal]**. Then it was time to go. I will never forget that day.

And was the only language resource used to form clause-complexes. Instead of signaling additive enhancement, the expected use for *and* in clause-complex formation, in five instances it was a temporal marker. The clause that follows the *and* is connected with the previous by time sequence. In two cases, it seems to be expressing causality: "I relaxed <u>because</u> she pulled me around."

Instructed genres

Different content areas called for instruction in different genres, thus Personal Recounts and Autobiographies were included in the English Language Arts (ELA) classes, Exposition in ELA and History, Procedures, Procedural Recounts, Reports, and Explanations in Science, and Parables in Religion.

In addition to the relationships present in the UPRs, during instruction students produced more relationships and at an earlier grade. Even Personal Recounts as part of ELA instruction showed use of additional relationships such as comparative and conditional. Procedural Recounts, Reports, and Explanations in Science gave students the opportunity to express new relationships such as adversative extensions, causal of purpose, conditional, and concessive.

The following science Report was written by the same fourth grader:

> The Beauties of the Tropical Rain Forest
>
> Tropical Rain Forests are very wet and warm. Thousands of species live in Tropical Rain Forests. Tropical Rain Forests are also very colorful.
>
> Animals
>
> All kinds of animals live in the Tropical Rain Forest. Some of them are monkeys and sloths. Monkeys are excellent climbers <u>because</u> they have long arms and strong hands. Sloths are slow-moving animals that usually spend several days <u>living in a single tree</u>.
>
> Plants
>
> Many plants grow in the Tropical Rain Forest. Some of them are the Obeche tree and the Banana tree. The Obeche tree can tower up to 60 meters <u>and</u> grow up to 7 meters wide. Banana trees aren't really trees at all. They're really giant herbs that can grow up to 306 meters!
>
> Climate
>
> <u>Since</u> Tropical Rain Forests are near the equator, they are warm all year. The air is very humid Tropical Rain Forests may get 80 to 4000 inches of rain a year.

The student expressed an additive relation with *and.* She also expressed causality using *because* and *since*. In addition, she used a non-finite clause to express manner.

This same student used an adversative in her Science Explanation: *One piece of bread was damp || while the other piece of bread was dry* and a conditional relationship: *If you put the water on a piece of bread, | it will eventually decay.*

Parables and Autobiographies also included adversative relations. The only example of elaboration appeared in Exposition, *It's almost | like they aren't committed to what they wrote* (MM, 7th, ND).

Development of logico-semantic relations and genres

The relationships appeared at different stages of development when comparing the UPRs and the instructed genres (Table 2.3). A number emerged in an earlier grade in the instructed genres while a few—typically found in early stages of development—appeared first in the UPRs.

Table 2.3. First appearance of logico-semantic relationships

First appearance in UPRs	Grade	First appearance in instructed genres
Additive Temporal	4	Adversative Causal (reason) Conditional (positive) Concessive
Projection Causal (reason) Spatial	5	Projection (locution) Adversative Variation
Adversative Variation	6	Causal (purpose) Conditional (positive) Concessive
	7	Projection (idea) Additive Temporal Causal (reason) Clarification
Concessive	8	Comparative Conditional (positive)

Procedural Recounts, Reports, and Explanations in Science gave fourth graders the opportunity to express relationships not usually expected at that young age such as adversative extensions, causal not only of reason but of purpose, conditional, and concessive. While adversative and variations were used in the UPRs in sixth grade, fifth grade writing already showed these relationships in Parables, Autobiographies, and Exposition, for example, *Why is people saying Happy Holidays || instead of saying Merry Christmas* (LL, 5th, Exposition, 12/20/11). Procedure writing in sixth grade led students to write concessive relationships, *You can make this by doing the same as mitochondria || except just use different colors* (CL, 11/14/11). These did not appear in the UPRs until eighth grade. Some relationships appeared first in the UPRs then in the other genres, such as projection (idea), causal (reason), temporal, and additive.

The types of relationships used in the instructed genres at the various grade levels do not seem to follow the developmental order found in the literature where additive, temporal, and causal of reason are the first to be used (Christie, 2010; Kress, 1982; Loban, 1976, Perera, 1984), but rather the use responds to the demands of the genre. For example, in fourth grade students wrote Science Explanations; such relations as causal, conditional, concessive, and adversative help develop the Explanation sequence. In the fifth graders' Parables, locutions in the form of quotes were abundant, *The younger daughter said to the father || "father where has our younger brother gone"* (KI, 5th, Parables,

10/24/11). Parables are characterized by moving the Narrative forward through dialogue among participants.

Dependency relationships

With respect to dependency, paratactic constructions were used by all students and with all types of logico-semantic relations. They were present in all genres, but particularly in the UPRs, where they often formed strings of paratactic sentences.

> This year I went to the park with my friend || and me and my friend were sitting down doing nothing || then we were watching this kid just shooting hoops || and he came up to us || and said || "do you want to play basketball with me" || so we said || yes ||| so he said || what game do you want to play || and we said || fifty fifty so he said || ok. (PN, 7th, Personal Recount, 12/19/11)

Hypotactic or dependent clauses were present in both types of projections but only in enhancement expansions (See Table 2.4). They appeared in both the UPRs and the other genres, but they were noticeably less frequent than paratactic constructions. The most common was dependent clauses expressing causality.

Table 2.4. Types of logico-semantic relations and dependency used by students

Logico-semantic relations		**Dependency**	
		Paratactic (equal or coordinate)	Hypotactic (subordinate)
Projection	Locution	✓	✓
	Idea	✓	✓
Expansion	Elaboration	✓	None
	Extension	✓	None
	Enhancement	✓	✓

Frequently, students expressed relations with the ubiquitous conjunction *and* creating a paratactic construction. A hypotactic construction could have made the meaning more clear and in some cases, the use of non-finite verbs, would have helped pack the writing (See Table 2.5).

Table 2.5. Paratactic and hypotactic equivalent

Students' writing	**Hypotactic equivalent**
I went to the zoo and I saw a hippo …	I went to the zoo where I saw a hippo … (elaboration)
We changed into our bathing suits and found a place to sit.	After we changed into our bathing suits, we found a place to sit (temporal).

It was the end of the 2011 school year and I was so happy	I was so happy because it was the end of the school year (causal).
The desert is extremely hot during the day and extremely cold in the night.	The desert is extremely hot during the day but extremely cold at night (concessive).
The water pulled us the whole way and water splashed everywhere.	The water pulled us the whole way, splashing everywhere (manner).

The data illustrated grade 4–8 students' attempts at expressing their ideas through a variety of clause-complexes. This transition stage between the grammar of oral and written language is characterized by favoring paratactic constructions and certain relationships such as projection and additive, temporal, and causal expansions as well as a limited number of conjunctive resources. Variation occurred with maturity and variation in genre writing.

Discussion

The purpose of this study was to analyze students' ability to express logico-semantic relations and to construct clause-complexes in a variety of genres. The results show that as students write in a variety of genres and progress in grade level they use more types of relations. In addition, difficulties with construction of dependent clauses (hypotaxis) impacted expression of relations.

Children were able to use a variety of logico-semantic relations. Students used an increasing number of relationships when they wrote UPRs as they advanced in grades. In fifth grade there was an explosion of new relations with a few new additions in sixth and eighth grades. However, a greater variety of relationships appeared among younger grades in the context of content instruction, especially Science. Projections were very common. They appeared both in UPRs and other genres in both paratactic and hypotactic structures. Of all the other relations, the most common were expansions that were additive, temporal, and causal (reason). Other research has indicated that these are common in written language at this age (Christie, 2010; Kress, 1982; Loban, 1976; Perera, 1984), while the majority of other logico-semantic relations tend to be used with greater frequency in high school (Loban, 1976; Myhill, 2008).

Challenges in constructing clause-complexes are also rooted in children's difficulties with hypotaxis (Christie & Derewianka, 2008). This struggle leads them to resort to the use of the ubiquitous *and*, thus indicating temporal, causal, and other dependent relations as parataxis. Moreover, the inability to use non-finite hypotactic clauses leads to wordy clause-complexes more typical of oral language. Evidence that these students had not yet made a full transition to the written language was also found in the strings of clauses connected with conjunctions such as *and*, *so*, *then*, and *and then*. These types of constructions were only present in their UPRs, suggesting that this genre itself, so prevalent in elementary schools, may lead to oral-like writing.

Clause-complexes pack "a great deal of information into a single intricately constructed sequence in a way which signals that it has been produced with careful, conscious planning" (Thompson, 2004, pp. 195–196) typical of written language. These types of constructions are different from spoken language, especially conversations, which tends to be loosely connected and typically unplanned. Compacting language decreases redundancy and increases lexical density as opposed to oral language where language resources are used to increase redundancy and decrease lexical density (Christie, 2010; Czerniewska, 1992). As children develop as writers the lexical density of their writing increases, and they begin to create more subordinate clauses (Hunt, 1965; Loban 1976). Analyzing clause-complexes in children's writing is one way to identify if their writing is becoming more like written language, rather than oral language written down. Among students in this study, UPR writing looked more like oral language than the coached writing in a variety of genres in connection to various disciplines.

Based on this study, the children's ability to use the clause-complex and express different logico-semantic relations, an important step in children's writing development, can be explained by children's ability to break from the temporal organization of clauses and to construct dependent clauses. In addition, practices that provide opportunities to write in a variety of genres in content area classes increase the chances of students trying different relationships. Even fourth graders can use relationships that are not commonly expected at this age (Hunt, 1965).

Implications for instruction

Teaching students to write means teaching the specific features of written language and of different genres. The results of this study suggest that students need instruction in logico-semantic relations other than additive, temporal, and causal. They need practice in hypotactic construction, often replacing the paratactic ones, including the ability to use non-finite verbs to pack their sentences. Much of this learning will emerge naturally by giving students the opportunity to write in a variety of genres across subject areas. Challenging students to write in genres beyond Personal Recounts requires them to express a variety of ideas and semantic relations leading to the construction of a range of types of clause-complexes in their writing. Temporal, additive, and causal relations are common in Personal Recounts. In some cases children also used projections to express speech or thinking, suggesting an opportunity to more explicitly instruct students in using dialogue in their Personal Recounts. Writing instruction in other genres and subject areas provides additional context for students to develop a variety of types of clause-complexes. Science Reports, Explanations, and Procedures require students to express adversative, concessive, and comparative relations at earlier grade levels and to formulate more hypotactic constructions. Further, children's tendency is to sequence clauses so that the linguistic order mirrors the temporal order of events. Different genres, such as Explanations or Expositions, encourage students to construct clause-complexes that rely on logical rather than temporal order.

The other benefit in expanding writing experiences beyond Personal Recounts is that it may facilitate the transition from oral to written language. The Personal Recounts, even in the upper grades, often had the characteristics of oral language written down with paratactic clauses joined by *and* or *so*. When students wrote in other genres, their texts had more characteristics of academic written language with more dependent clauses and more lexically dense sentences. Children would benefit from attention to differences in the discourse, text organization, vocabulary, and structure of oral and written language.

Giving students the opportunity to write in different genres does not preclude providing explicit instruction in how to construct clause-complexes, including the use of a variety of conjunctions, and alternatives to clause-complexes for a more packed language. This study is consistent with Hunt's (1965) findings that by fourth grade children are able to construct the various types of clause-complexes, although they do so infrequently. Apprenticing students to written language should include teaching how to express logico-semantic relations through well-constructed and meaningful clause-complexes. Children can be taught about the different connectives and shown the possibilities beyond the ubiquitous *and*. Through deconstruction of mentor texts, where these resources are used, students can begin to see the possibilities. Studying what published authors do can be followed by joint-construction of texts where the teacher can clarify what the students want to mean and show them how to do it with language. Further instruction can take place while conferencing with students after they have written their own independent pieces. By helping students construct clause-complexes they will be better able to express the complex relationships that they are ready to include in their writing.

References

Bloom, L., Lahey, M., Hood, L., Lifter, K., & Fiess, K. (1980). Complex sentences: Acquisition of syntactic connectives and the semantic relations they encode. *Journal of Child Language, 7*(2), 235–61. http://dx.doi.org/10.1017/S0305000900002610

Butt, D., Fahey, R., Feez, S., Spinks, S., & Yallop, C. (2000). *Using functional grammar: An explorer's guide* (2nd ed.). Sydney, Australia: National Centre for English Language Teaching and Research: Macquarie University.

Christie, F. (2010). The ontogenesis of writing in childhood and adolescence. In D. Wyse, R. Andrews and J. Hoffman (Eds.), *The international handbook of English, language and literacy teaching* (pp. 146–158). London: Routledge/Taylor and Francis.

Christie, F. (2012). *Language education throughout the school years: A functional perspective*. Chichester, West Sussex: Wiley-Blackwell.

Christie, F., & Derewianka, B. (2008). *School discourse: Learning to write across the years of schooling*. London: Continuum.

Czerniewska, P. (1992) *Learning about writing.* Oxford: Blackwell

Derewianka, B., & Jones, P. (2012). *Teaching language in context.* South Melbourne, Victoria: Oxford University Press.

Eisenberg, A. (1980). A syntactic, semantic and pragmatic analysis of conjunction. *Stanford Papers and Reports on Child Language Development, 19*, 70–78.

Eggins, S. (2004). *An introduction to systemic functional linguistics.* London: Continuum.

Halliday, M. A. K. (1989). *Spoken and written language*. Oxford: Oxford University Press.

Halliday, M. A. K. & Matthiessen, C. M. I. M. (2004). *An introduction to functional grammar* (3rd ed.). London: Hodder Arnold.

Hunt, K. W. (1965). *Grammatical structures written at three grade levels.* Champaign, IL: National Council of Teachers of English.

Katz, W. E., & Brent, S. (1968). Understanding connectives. *Journal of Verbal Learning and Verbal Behavior, 7*(2), 501–509. http://dx.doi.org/10.1016/S0022-5371(68)80040-4

Kress, G. (1982) *Learning to write*. London: Routledge.

Kroll, B. M., & Lempers, J. D. (1981). Effect of mode of communication on the information adequacy of children's explanations. *Journal of Genetic Psychology, 138*, 27–35.

Loban, W. (1976) *Language development: Kindergarten through grade twelve.* Research Report 18. Urbana, IL: National Council of Teachers of English.

Lull, H. G. (1929). The speaking and writing abilities of intermediate grade pupils. *Journal of Educational Research, 20*, 73–77.

Myhill, D. (2008). Towards a linguistic model of sentence development in writing. *Language and Education, 22*(5), 271–288. http://dx.doi.org/10.1080/09500780802152655

National Commission on Writing. (2003). *The neglected R: The need for a writing revolution.* Retrieved from www.collegeboard.com

National Commission on Writing. (2005). *Writing: A powerful message from state government.* Retrieved from www.collegeboard.com

Perera, K. (1984). *Children's writing and reading: Analysing classroom language.* Oxford: Blackwell.

Spooren, W., & Sanders, T. (2008). The acquisition order of coherence relations: On cognitive complexity in discourse. *Journal of Pragmatics, 40*(12), 2003–2026. http://dx.doi.org/10.1016/j.pragma.2008.04.021

Thompson, G. (2004). *Introducing functional grammar* (2nd ed.). London: Arnold.

3 Tackling a genre: situating SFL genre pedagogy in a new context

Mary J. Schleppegrell, Jason Moore, Shireen Al-Adeimi, Catherine L. O'Hallaron, Annemarie Sullivan Palincsar, and Carrie Symons

The systemic functional linguistics (SFL) model of genre developed in Australia has begun to influence the work of researchers and teachers across the U.S.A. who have become interested in its potential to support literacy instruction. In particular, the work of the Sydney School (see Martin, 1993 for an overview), with its careful analysis and description of students' writing across grades and disciplines in Australia, offers valuable models and pedagogical approaches that can inform writing instruction in other contexts. However, in drawing on any model from another context, issues inevitably emerge which call for modifications to suit the specific features, stakeholders, and culture of the new context. This chapter discusses the issues we confronted as we worked to implement genre-based writing in a U.S. school district with a large number of English language learners (ELLs). In this context we had to grapple with contextual and pedagogical issues that shaped the genres that we scaffolded and our understanding of how best to support genre-based writing instruction. This is not surprising, as genres are social processes, not static products. Since the SFL framework enables us to consider the purposes, organizational structure potential, and relevance of particular language choices of a genre being scaffolded, it offers a means of flexibly adapting genre descriptions to particular contexts. In this chapter we report on how we developed and supported the writing of a genre that had affordances for particular purposes in our context and identify issues that emerged as we analyzed classroom interaction and students' written products. Our experience shows that the SFL genre approach offers a powerful yet flexible framework for presenting new genres in ways that are relevant to particular contexts and settings.

Context

The context for the work described here is an urban fringe high poverty school district in the Midwestern U.S.A., where we engaged in a three-year research project in schools with a majority population of bilingual students and many ELLs. Our goal was to use the tools of SFL to develop approaches and materials to support teachers in engaging ELLs in talk about language and meaning that would support their English language development. Initially, our application of SFL had emerged from concerns that the current reading program was helping children in the early grades decode and read with apparent fluency, but their comprehension was lagging far behind what was expected (Moore, Carlisle, & Schleppegrell, 2009). Our application of SFL was originally in support of students' comprehension of disciplinary texts in English Language Arts (ELA). Over time, however, teachers and administrators began to ask for more support for their writing instruction, in particular, to support argumentative writing tasks that the children had to perform during annual standardized assessments.

A design-based research approach (Bradley & Reinking, 2008; McKenney & Reeves, 2012) enabled us to investigate the challenges of authentic classroom contexts as we developed our approach to writing. In our first year of research (2010–2011), we worked closely with eight teachers at a pilot school. This experience helped us to understand the local learning context and informed the development of our approach. The next year, we expanded our project into five schools and worked with 21 teachers and instructional coaches to implement a more developed functional grammar approach that included genre-based writing pedagogy. The lessons were implemented in 12 classrooms serving approximately 300 students in grades 2–5. The student writing, pedagogical materials, and classroom observations from this work inform our reflections about the genre-based work presented in this chapter.

Every research and pedagogical context has its particular constraints on the ways researchers can work with teachers. In our case, local constraints shaped (a) the genres we took up and worked with, (b) how those genres were named and staged, and (c) the language features we focused on. In our context, the key challenge of applying the Australian genre approach has been developing genre descriptions to support the kinds of writing valued in the local context, taking into account established expectations and pedagogies as well as teachers' perspectives on language, grammar, and genre.

While the Sydney School work describes a range of pedagogical genres, the point of departure for making decisions about new curricular interventions needs to be the context of the curriculum in which the genre will be introduced. So our work began by reviewing the local curriculum goals and standards and learning about the writing that was already going on in our project schools and the ways teachers were supporting development of that writing.

The U.S. educational context is guided by learning standards, typically assessed by standardized tests. In our research site, teachers were accountable to district and state standards that list skills students need to develop. Such standards do not preclude a genre-based approach, but the skills delineated in the standards needed to be folded into the genre approach and explicitly addressed. State guidelines specifying grade-level content expectations list genres students should read and write by grade 8 (age 13), divided into two crude categories, "narrative" and "informational." At the schools, *genre* was a term used by teachers and students to "name" different text types (e.g., Tall Tale, Legend, Memoir, Myth) during reading instruction. The writing genres were mainly general and devoid of social purpose (e.g, Essay, Report), and the schools used a commercial program for writing instruction that offered teachers generic scaffolds.

We identified three writing tasks students were already doing that were relevant to our goals in helping teachers work with students on reading and comprehending stories in their literature programs. One writing task was called a Retell, which can be described as a chronological summary of a story's events absent of interpretive commentary or evaluation. The implied purpose of the task was for students to demonstrate to the teacher basic understanding of a text. We wanted to draw on convergences with that task that could be exploited in the new genre we would scaffold.

Teachers also often supported students to write non-chronological, topic-driven responses for various purposes. Such writing, regardless of topic or purpose, was often supported with generic writing scaffolds, such as a Topic-Detail organizer that provided boxes for a topic, three details, and a concluding sentence. Such scaffolds were used to support students' preparation for the state-administered standardized test of writing proficiency, which posed *Writing from knowledge and experience* prompts that were often about a specific theme; for example, "Each of us has special abilities. Describe something that makes you special. How do you use that ability?"

Students also engaged in different kinds of persuasive writing tasks, also supported by the same Topic-Detail scaffold. At the pilot school, persuasive writing was an official part of the school's yearly improvement plan. Each month, the school held a writing contest for which all students responded to prompts addressing debates relevant to students' lives; for example, writing letters to the principal to argue for new playground equipment. Such attempts at supporting students to write persuasively were often based on (assumed) common knowledge or personal experience, rather than academic content. Our experience in this context gave us insights into why the generic writing scaffolds were so universally applied.

However, when students shifted to academic writing in the content areas, generic scaffolds were not successful at supporting their attempts at argumentation. For example, the initial year of our project explored ways SFL could support students' reading of and conversations about literature, and we collaborated with teachers to develop writing prompts related to those conversations, but did not provide genre-specific guidance for writing. Instead, teachers used the Topic-Detail handout. In her analysis of these written products, O'Hallaron (2014) reported that very few students supported in this way attempted to analyze the details provided in their responses, only listing them but not relating them to their argument. Teachers and administrators at project schools were interested in additional support for argument writing and were receptive to more explicit and purposeful scaffolding of genres for their ELLs.

Exploring supportive and relevant SFL genres

Arguments in different school subjects have different social purposes, organizational structures, and ways of arguing realized by distinct language features, so we designed our genre-based approach to scaffold students to write specific types of argument common to disciplines, as identified by SFL theory (Christie & Derewianka, 2008; Martin & Rose, 2008). In the context of English Language Arts, we identified Character Analysis as a target genre. A Character Analysis is a common literary response genre that asks students to explain how a character changed and why, or to evaluate a character's words or actions for a particular purpose. This genre, however, is more common to secondary English classes, and presents many new challenges to younger students (Christie & Derewianka, 2008). Instead of summarizing events from a story, students need to make judgments about characters and carefully select relevant evidence in the form of characters' actions, dialogue, or attitudes, before commenting on how the evidence reveals aspects of the character's personality. This requires a level of inferential thinking not required for a simple summary of events.

We noted that the writing students were doing in the early years of schooling (e.g., Personal Response and Review) did not strongly support students' writing of Character Analysis. In fact, some features of personal responses (such as presentation of affective attitudes) that surface in students' attempts at analytical writing are negatively evaluated by teachers (Rothery & Stenglin, 2000). Thus, considering the significant number of new challenges presented by the target genre, we sought to teach an "antecedent genre," as described by Devitt (2004), who argues that "the genres teachers choose as illustrations or as writing assignments may become part of students' genre repertoires, become available to them as antecedents for learning new genres, and inculcate in them particular perceptions of situations" (pp. 202–203). We sought to present an antecedent genre that could serve as a bridge from the familiar retell task to more challenging analytical writing. Our goal was to present a genre that would ask students to summarize important events from a story chronologically, but also push them to make inferences about characters' attitudes and provide evaluative comments about the characters.

We drew on descriptions of Recount/Account genres in history (e.g., Coffin, 2006), seeing these as related to retelling events from a story text, and on Biographical Recount, where students have to write about and evaluate a historical character using two main stages, Orientation and Record of Events, with an optional Evaluation (Coffin, 2006, p. 54). A related genre is described in Martin and Rose (2003, p. 8) as an Exemplum, whose social purpose is to "present a problematic incident and then interpret it for the audience, commenting on the behaviour of the people involved."

Bringing these together, we supported the teaching of a genre we called a Recount. This differed both from the retell that teachers were already familiar with and also from the Sydney School Recount models for history and for retelling personal experience. We conceived of the Recount in our context as a genre connected with retelling events in a story rather than retelling personal experience, and presented it to teachers as a pedagogical genre that would support children in analyzing characters in a story in preparation for thesis-driven writing. Our hope was that the Recount would add to their repertoire of genres, serving as an especially rich antecedent genre to Character Analysis. By having the children purposefully retell important events, interpret characters' feelings, and provide an evaluative comment, we had the goal of supporting them in learning to draw on what they read in ways that could then be used to accomplish the Character Analysis genre that we planned to support in our next unit.

In this way we wanted to help students write about a story in ways that connected with and extended writing they were already doing in their curricular context, but also aligned with what our own approach aimed to accomplish, explicitly linked to the state and district standards. By exploring the current practices and needs of the context, we were better equipped to purposefully modify the Sydney School genre descriptions for local pedagogical goals. The following section reviews how the Recount genre was developed and presented in our research context.

Defining the Recount genre for our context

When introducing a new genre, the overall purpose needs to be made clear, and the purposes established for each stage need to enable a coherent response across the text as a whole. Our formulation of the purpose of the Recount was that it should "tell about a series of events in order to report on a character's actions or feelings or to show how the character develops during the story and to comment on why that's important." The stages and language features were presented as follows:

1. The *Orientation* gives the person who reads the Recount important background information about the character and when or where the events take place. The first sentence of a Recount usually includes a *Circumstance of time* or a *Circumstance of place* to present this background information (related to the purpose of the Orientation.)
2. The *Sequence of Events* tells what happened, in order. In the Sequence of Events, any kind of process can be used, but the most common kinds are *doing* and *sensing* processes to talk about a character's actions or feelings.
3. The *Evaluation* says why these events were important. It *makes a judgment about the events and/or says why these events were important or interesting.* The Evaluation usually has a *being* or *sensing* Process that helps you comment on the story by judging the events and/or saying what's interesting or important about them.

We attempted to reinforce the purpose and stages of the genre through a writing prompt, which is crucial in articulating expectations of the genre to students. The prompt needs to support the genre being modeled while also being specific and relevant to the story addressed. The fourth grade lessons focused on Pat Mora's story *Tomás and the Library Lady* (1997). The main character Tomás, the son of migrant farm workers, loves to listen to his grandfather's stories. His grandfather encourages Tomás to go the library, where the librarian befriends him. He falls in love with reading and becomes the newest storyteller in his family. The writing prompt was: *In the story* Tomás and the Library Lady, *Tomás becomes the newest storyteller in his family. Re-tell some of the most important events in the story, how Tomás felt, and how they relate to his becoming a storyteller.*

Overview of our genre-based writing pedagogy

We situated the genre teaching in the local curriculum by introducing the Recount task as the final product of a unit in which students read and discussed a story from the reading curriculum. Along with genre descriptions, the Sydney School is also known for its pedagogical approach to teaching writing, represented by the teaching-learning cycle of *text deconstruction, joint construction*, and *independent construction* (e.g., Martin, 1999). Our instructtional approach incorporated these elements, but our approach had to be integrated with other literacy instruction practices in the classrooms as our learning goals also focused on supporting reading comprehension.

After four days of professional development, teachers implemented the unit and we observed their classrooms as they taught the lessons we had designed. Students first learned to apply constructs from Appraisal theory (Martin & White, 2005) to recognize how the language of a story can convey characters' attitudes (see Moore & Schleppegrell, 2014). Multiple lessons were devoted to analysis of the story before teachers moved into the scaffolding of the Recount genre and supporting students in writing. In introducing the genre, teachers analyzed a model Recount with the students, identifying the stages and language features (using the SFL constructs *Processes and Circumstances* of different kinds) before having the children write drafts of the Recount. Students reviewed their writing with peers to consider how they had achieved the stages and their purposes, and then wrote final versions. These activities took about two weeks of Language Arts class time.

Learning from implementation

In this section we discuss how analysis of student writing and videotapes of lesson implementation helped us identify affordances and limitations of our genre-based approach. We first present examples of the children's writing, and then address issues related to stating the overall purpose of the genre, its stages and language features, and the supporting prompts. We analyzed the writing from each classroom, focusing on the ways students realized the various stages and looking at the overall coherence of the Recount texts. One aspect of the writing that raised important issues for us was the variation in student writing within and across the classrooms. To further explore this issue, we reviewed the materials we provided teachers, as well as videos of classroom implementation. Our analysis identifies challenges, tensions and dilemmas that surfaced in our work, but the affordances show that SFL genres are dynamic and adaptive to local contexts, and can support students' writing in challenging, highly valued ways.

Figures 3.1 and 3.2 provide examples of Recounts written by two fourth grade students in the same class, both of whom speak Arabic as a first language. Figure 3.1, written by Yasmin, is a successful attempt at the Recount, as judged by the researchers. Figure 3.2, by Adam, is less successful (names are pseudonyms).

On the days that Tomás is with Papa Grande in Iowa, Papa Grande says some things that inspire him to become a storyteller. Tomás does some things that inspire him too.

One of the most important events in the story that show how Tomás felt and relates to him becoming a storyteller is Tomás with Papa Grande under a tree. In that event Tomas felt happy, pleased, and excited. This relates to him becoming a story teller because Papa Grande told Tomás "he is old enough to go to the library." If Papa Grande did'nt tell him to go to the library, Tomás would not have become a storyteller.

Another event is Tomás starts reading. In this event, he felt excited, interested, and engaged in his book. This relates to him becoming a storyteller because he starts to read new books and he starts to imagine his book. He imagined "dinousours lapping water."

These events were important and interesting because they both show many feelings and they both relate to him becoming a storyteller. Tomás loved being the new storyteller in his family.

Figure 3.1 Writing sample from Yasmin

Transcript of Figure 3.1:

On the days that Tomás is with Papa Grande in Iowa, Papa Grande says some things that inspire him to become a storyteller. Tomás does some things that inspire him too.

One of the most important events in the story that show how Tomás felt and relates to him becoming a storyteller is Tomás with Papa Grande under a tree. In that event Tomas felt happy, pleased, and excited. This relates to him becoming a story teller because Papa Grande told Tomás "he is old enough to go to the library." If Papa Grande did'nt tell him to go to the library, Tomás would not have become a storyteller.

Another event is Tomás starts reading. In this event, he felt excited, interested, and engaged in his book. This relates to him becoming a storyteller because he starts to read new books and he starts to imagine his book. He imagined "dinousours lapping water."

These events were important and interesting because they both show many feelings and they both related to him becoming a storyteller. Tomás loved being the new storyteller in his family.

Yasmin connects to the storyteller theme across stages. The Orientation provides an overview that sets up the writing task effectively. Then, using the work she and the class had done in identifying and analyzing Tomás's feelings, she presents two key events, relates them to the storyteller theme, and both comments on them and tells us how Tomás felt about becoming a storyteller in her Evaluation.

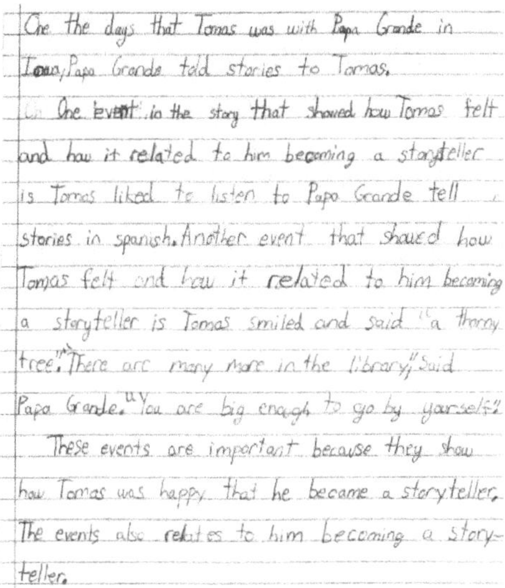
On the days that Tomas was with Papa Grande in Iowa, Papa Grande told stories to Tomas.

One event in the story that showed how Tomas felt and how it related to him becoming a storyteller is Tomas liked to listen to Papo Grande tell stories in spanish. Another event that shaued how Tomas felt and how it related to him becoming a storyteller is Tomas smiled and said "a thorny tree." "There are many more in the library," Said Papa Grande. "You are big enough to go by yourself."

These events are important because they show how Tomas was happy that he became a storyteller. The events also relates to him becoming a storyteller.

Figure 3.2. Writing sample from Adam

Transcript of Figure 3.2:

> On the days that Tomás was with Papa Grande in Iowa, Papa Grande told stories to Tomás.
>
> One event in the story that showed how Tomás felt and how it related to him becoming a storyteller is Tomás liked to listen to Papa Grande tell stories in Spanish. Another event that showed how Tomás felt and how it related to him becoming a storyteller is Tomas smiled and said "a thorny tree." "There are many more in the library," said Papa Grande. "You are big enough to go by yourself."
>
> These events are important because they show how Tomás was happy that he became a storyteller. The events also relates to him becoming a storyteller.

Adam's Orientation gives background that connects loosely to the storytelling theme but he does not introduce it directly. He includes two events that introduce the notion of Tomás becoming a storyteller and report on how Tomás felt (*liked to listen*; *smiled*), but the relevance of the events is unclear. The reader needs more information to understand what is referred to. In his Evaluation, Adam ties back to the prompt but in fact he has not shown how Tomás is happy, as the events are not elaborated enough. This showed us that some students needed more help introducing, elaborating, and drawing significance from events they chose to report on.

Below we address issues that emerged in our analysis of students' writing that are relevant for understanding what is needed to support the presentation of a new genre. These include being clear about the purpose of the genre as a whole and issues in the writing of prompts, as well as providing support for creating coherence across stages of the genre, including making the purpose of each stage clear and identifying relevant language features. We use discussion of these issues to highlight concerns that need to be taken into account in the introduction of new genres within a genre-based pedagogy.

In stating the purpose for the Recount ("to tell about a series of events in order to report on a character's actions or feelings or to show how the character develops during the story and to comment on why that's important"), we see now that our focus was too diffuse, with four areas foregrounded: events, a character's actions, a character's feelings, and a character's development. While these areas are all related, listing them all makes the overall purpose less clear. In addition, asking students to comment on "why that's important" is quite general. Recognizing these points has helped us see that the purpose of a Recount is likely to vary, depending on the aspect of the story in focus and the purposes for retelling part of the story, as students could be asked to recount events that relate to a range of issues.

The central tension here is between that of the competing purposes of the Recount genre and our own pedagogical ones. The Recount genre is focused on important events that are relevant to a topic. The evaluation of those events involves discussing why they deepen or complicate one's understanding of the topic. For example, one might recount the story of *Tomás* in order to make the point that reading can help one escape from the challenges of real life, or that finding a natural talent, such as storytelling, can be important to one's self-esteem and happiness. Such commentaries require making inferences about the character, but the focus and purpose for the Recount is not necessarily squarely centered on the character. However, in preparing students for Character Analysis, we attempted to shift the focus of the Recount genre onto the characters. This tension highlights the importance of closely considering the overall social purposes of the antecedent genre as well as the target genre, carefully considering the ways they are complementary and what kind of variation each supports.

As we were unaware of these competing, but very related purposes, our prompts sometimes lacked the clarity necessary to scaffold students in the task. For example, the *Tomás* prompt asks students to report on the "most important events," on "how he felt," and "why he felt that way." But the main purpose for reporting these is to write about "how it relates to his becoming a storyteller." This wording and organization of the prompt did not support the organizational structure we scaffolded for the genre as a whole. In retrospect, we recognize that the point of retelling events, to write about how Tomás became a "storyteller," should be foregrounded, with the points about events and feelings in service of that goal, as students need to focus on events and feelings that relate to becoming a storyteller. While not all genres would necessarily confront the issue—since this is a tension between competing purposes of the antecedent and target genres—it is nevertheless something to consider in thinking about the relationship between purpose and prompt, as the two need to be closely linked.

Our attempts to simplify the task for younger students also posed challenges for keeping the writing purpose front and center. For example, one of our prompts asked students to recount events only from one episode of a story. We considered this more appropriate for introducing young children (seven-year-olds) to their first Recount task. This worked well for recounting what the main character was doing at a particular moment in the story, but it did not help students focus on a larger point for writing.

Our current understanding of this Recount task is that the purpose should be stated in a way that foregrounds the fact that there will be different reasons for recounting events; e.g., the purpose of a Recount is to tell about a series of events *to provide a judgment or comment on a specific topic*. Our more generic purpose statement, then, can be paired with prompts that are specific to particular stories. This realization has also led us to reconsider Recount's role as an antecedent genre to Character Analysis. Several features of the Recount we still see as beneficial to preparing students for analytical writing, for example, as retelling of events includes inferences about a character's emotional reactions to those events. However, we found that the evaluative final stage of Recount (commentary on events in relation to a topic) was qualitatively different than Evaluations needed in Character Analyses (evaluative statements about characters in relation to a topic). Moving forward, as we use Recount as an antecedent genre to Character Analysis, we will take account of these findings to inform the supporting pedagogy, including being mindful of the ways different prompts support different kinds of responses.

The writing analysis also showed us that our support for creating coherence across the Recount stages needed to be strengthened. In reviewing our materials, we saw that while our overall stated purpose focused on character development, the stage descriptions emphasized events. We realized that the stage descriptions needed to be more closely in service of the overall purpose in order to support greater cohesion across the text.

In the Orientation stage, students often focused on providing the reader with background information about the time and place of the story—that Tomás had moved to Iowa for the summer. However, students did not orient the reader to the overall purpose of the writing by introducing the notion of *becoming a storyteller*. This could partially be traced back to our lesson and the supporting materials, which emphasized the language features *circumstances of time/place*, but did not provide enough support for setting up the point to be carried through over the stages of the Recount. Some students did write Orientations that achieved this goal, as we see in Yasmin's writing, but others did not.

How much of the story and which parts of the story are to be retold in the Sequence of Events stage is also shaped by the overall purpose of the writing. This stage was more challenging for students than we had anticipated, as the selection of events has to be considered in relation to the purpose for writing. In the context of this prompt, the "important events" are those happenings in the story that were critical to Tomás's development into his family's newest storyteller. Students struggled to select important events across a story and with how much detail to include.

The Evaluation stage was realized in very different ways across classrooms, leading us to rethink the functional purposes and what we wanted students to accomplish with this stage. Our stated purpose for the Evaluation stage was "to make a judgment about the events reported," but the texts that students actually produced included other purposes in this stage as well: telling why the events are important, telling how the character felt, and writing about who influenced the character. In some cases the students did not link back to the key point from the prompt. Teachers felt that students needed some transition to the Evaluation stage, and we saw them scaffold this in a variety of ways. In several classes the majority of the Evaluations began with some kind of sentence frame: *This shows ...*; *These events are important because ...* We now recognize how our own competing expectations for the purpose of the genre led to different realizations of Evaluation. We learned from the different ways teachers provided support that made the expectations for this stage clearer for the students and from the different kinds of evaluative judgments students made of the events, the characters, or the characters' feelings, and saw that the genre provided opportunities for them to learn to respond to texts in more analytical ways.

A key aspect of SFL support for genre-based instruction is a focus on language features that students can attend to in both reading and writing. This reading-writing link, made through classroom talk about the story being written about and the genre being constructed, was an important focus of our professional development. In classroom implementation we saw the value of identifying particular language features related to each stage, but our analysis shows us that we need to link the features being foregrounded more clearly to the overall purpose and the purpose for each stage. For example, while a focus on *Circumstances of time and place* is valuable in supporting students in writing the Orientation stage, it is not sufficient. The value of the metalanguage is clearly illustrated in classroom talk that shows that being able to provide concrete guidance to students about *how to get started* is helpful. In one second grade classroom, for example, the teacher asked the children how they had started the stories they wrote the previous week. All of the student responses focused on form rather than meaning (e.g., a capital letter, a title). In contrast, talk about an Orientation and the metalanguage of *Circumstances of time and place* were useful in guiding them about "how to begin" in more meaning-focused ways. Later, when the children were giving each other feedback on their Recounts, they looked for Circumstances of time and place in their Orientations, thus providing some content for a writing process activity.

While the explicit focus on language features was useful in these ways, it was not sufficient for supporting Orientation to the writer's *purpose*. The focus on Circumstances did not align with the full purpose of the stage, where students also need to set up the reason for writing, not simply tell where and when the story took place. In our advice about the Orientation, the language features highlighted something that was not central to the purpose, as the Orientation in a Recount needs to be to the topic or character, rather than to time/place. Recognizing this helped us understand that the language features need to support the larger purpose of each stage.

The language features introduced also need to be specific enough to be useful. In the Sequence of Events stage, we had introduced the SFL notions of *Processes of different types* to help the children read and understand how characters' feelings were presented in the stories they read. They learned that character's feelings are not only presented in their *sensing* and *being* Processes, but also in their *doing* and *saying* Processes, where authors *show* how characters feel instead of directly *telling* (Moore & Schleppegrell, 2014). While this was helpful in supporting their reading and interpretation of the story, our advice about Processes in the Sequence of Events stage, where we suggested using *sensing* to report a character's feelings and *doing* to report events, was less useful. In retrospect, we see that in fact all four Process types are important for reporting events, and that we need to focus more strategically on language features to be helpful to students.

The notion of genre-based writing has been generative for our work with teachers, providing purpose for re-reading and analyzing a text as well as "content" for writing instruction to support curricular goals. In addition, the functional metalanguage offered new ways of talking explicitly about expectations for writing. Teachers were generally pleased with the Recount unit. On reflection logs (1 = strongly disagree and 4 = strongly agree), they reported average ratings of 3 on how functional grammar helped their students talk about text, comprehend text and compose a written piece, indicating an overall positive response to the learning their students experienced. In interviews, they reported that teaching the Recount offered them new ways to support students through writing instruction, and that the metalanguage gave them new ways to be explicit with students about what to write.

Implications and discussion

To focus teachers and students on genre as choice in context for particular purposes, we need to foreground disciplinary perspectives and help teachers accomplish goals they already have for students' learning. In this project we focused on ELA goals that can help students move toward the analytical writing they will need to do in middle and secondary school, supporting emergent kinds of analysis of characters that build toward that goal. Key principles that shape the choices made in introducing and supporting genres include attention to what the larger goals of the activity are, a focus on choice in context, and metalanguage for talking about language choices. A genre-based approach can support writing in rhetorical ways with meaningful and carefully targeted focus on language features that enable the purposes. Identifying appropriate language features calls for work in developing meaningful metalanguage within the classroom context so the metalanguage can serve as a means of talking about the meaning in texts rather than just as a labeling exercise.

Genres are ever evolving and not static, and, in work with teachers, genre descriptions need to be adapted to local contexts so that they serve larger curricular purposes and are discipline-specific. The development and evolution of our genre-based writing program demonstrates the flexibility and usefulness of an approach that draws on the Sydney School research and develops genre descriptions focused on purpose, stages, and language features. The notion of genre as social process is key here, as the genre approach is not in service of teaching "a genre," but instead about teaching a process of construing meaning purposefully in writing. This is also true of our pedagogical process in identifying a meaningful genre and supporting teachers in scaffolding students' ability to write that genre. Sydney School descriptions cannot be brought into new contexts and taught as "things," but need to be adapted by considering the kind of writing that teachers in a particular context want to support and then developing that support through a process of identifying purposes, stages, and language features, embedding the writing in a pedagogical context that is relevant to the local classroom ecology, and then studying implementation and students' products to continue to refine and develop the supports.

Acknowledgment

We thank the teachers and children we have worked with for their many contributions to the work presented here. The research reported here was supported by the Institute of Education Sciences, U.S. Department of Education, through Grant R305A100482 to the University of Michigan. The opinions expressed are those of the authors and do not represent views of the Institute or the U.S. Department of Education.

References

Bradley, B. A., & Reinking, D. (2008). Enhancing research and practice in early childhood through formative and design experiments. *Early Child Development and Care, 181*(3), 305–319. http://dx.doi.org/10.1080/03004430903357894

Christie, F., & Derewianka, B. (2008). *School discourse: Learning to write across the years of schooling*. London: Continuum.

Coffin, C. (2006). *Historical discourse: The language of time, cause, and evaluation.* London: Continuum.

Devitt, A. J. (2004). *Writing genres*. Carbondale: Southern Illinois University Press.

Martin, J. R. (1993). Genre and literacy—Modeling context in educational linguistics. *Annual Review of Applied Linguistics, 13*, 141–172. http://dx.doi.org/10.1017/S0267190500002440

Martin, J. R. (1999). Mentoring semogenesis: "Genre-based" literacy pedagogy. In F. Christie (Ed.), *Pedagogy and the shaping of consciousness: Linguistic and social processes* (pp. 123–155). London: Continuum.

Martin, J. R., & Rose, D. (2003). *Working with discourse*. London: Continuum.

Martin, J. R., & Rose, D. (2008). *Genre relations: Mapping culture*. Oakville, CT: Equinox.

Martin, J. R., & White, P. R. R. (2005). *The language of evaluation*. New York: Palgrave Macmillan.

McKenney, S., & Reeves, T. (2012). *Conducting educational design research*. New York: Routledge.

Moore, J. P., Carlisle, J. F., & Schleppegrell, M. J. (2009). *Reading achievement of English language learners in Reading First Schools in Michigan* (Technical Report #7.3). Ann Arbor, MI: University of Michigan.

Moore, J., & Schleppegrell, M. J. (2014). Using a functional linguistics metalanguage to support academic language development in the English Language Arts. *Linguistics and Education 26*, 92–105. http://dx.doi.org/10.1016/j.linged.2014.01.002

Mora, P. (1997). *Tomás and the library lady*. New York: Random House.

O'Hallaron, C. (2014). Supporting fifth-grade ELLs' argumentative writing development. *Written Communication 31*, 304–331. http://dx.doi.org/10.1177/0741088314536524

Rothery, J., & Stenglin, M. (2000). Interpreting literature: The role of appraisal. In L. Unsworth (Ed.), *Researching language in schools and communities* (pages 222–244). London: Cassell.

4 Elementary grade teachers using systemic functional linguistics to inform genre-based writing instruction

Frank Daniello

High-quality writing instruction must begin in the early years of schooling, as writing proficiency is a foundational skill required for learning, college, and career readiness. However, over the past decade, educators have expressed concern with the quality of writing instruction (see National Commission on Writing, 2003). This concern continues to be voiced (see Cutler & Graham, 2008; Gilbert & Graham, 2010; Graham & Harris, 2013). Results from the National Assessment of Educational Progress (NAEP) in 2011 indicated that of the sampled eighth (N = 24,100) and twelfth (N = 28,100) grade students only 24% performed at the *proficient* level (National Center for Education Statistics, 2012). The majority of assessed eighth (54%) and twelfth (52%) grade students performed at the *basic* level in writing. This signifies only partial mastery of the required skills and knowledge to work successfully at each grade level. Results from NAEP (2011), in conjunction with expressed concern from educators, suggest that improvements are needed to the teaching of writing in the U.S.A.

Research indicates that writing instruction in elementary schools consists mostly of activities involving writing to learn: short answer responses, completing worksheets, writing in content areas, note taking, and writing to summarize (Gilbert & Graham, 2010). These activities are educationally valuable, but the teaching of writing must also involve students writing for various purposes. Presently, this does not occur in all classes within a school or systemically across all schools in the U.S.A. For example, little instructional attention is given to persuasive and report writing (Gilbert & Graham, 2010).

This chapter describes a longitudinal case study that examined changes to the content of fourth and fifth grade teachers' genre-based writing pedagogy over a three-year period. The teachers in these grades taught in a traditionally underperforming urban elementary school located in a city in Massachusetts. They participated in a school–university partnership that focused on assisting teachers with using systemic functional linguistics (SFL) to understand genre in order to improve classroom writing instruction. Study findings illustrate ways the teachers operationalized this theory of language in their writing instruction with students to teach genre.

Genre from a social semiotic perspective

SFL provides a lens to study genre from a social semiotic perspective (Halliday, 1994; Halliday & Hasan, 1989). SFL identifies language as a "set of resources for making meaning, rather than rules for ordering structures" (Rose & Martin, 2012, p. 21). As stated in the introduction of this book, according to this theory, language usage is contingent on context of culture and context of situation (Butt et al., 2000; Eggins, 1994).

The context of culture determines how language is used to achieve a genre. For example, in Asian cultures, persuasive texts are staged differently than in Anglo-American cultures. Both cultures seek to persuade, but use language differently to achieve this social goal. In Asian-based persuasive texts, the purpose is "delayed until the end of the piece of writing, causing it to be inductive rather than deductive … the goal of such discourse organization is to convince the reader of the validity of the writer's position and lead the audience to support the writer's stance, instead of employing overt persuasion, which may be considered to be excessively direct and forceful" (Hinkel, 2002, p. 31).

In Anglo-American texts, overt persuasion is practiced and used to influence the reader to embrace the writer's stance. This stylistic comparison shows how language use in genre varies across two cultures, despite both forms seeking similar social purposes. The context of situation is nested in the context of culture and represents the social dimensions that affect linguistics (Butt et al., 2000; Eggins, 1994; Halliday & Hasan, 1989) and makes up the register. The register is enacted through three metafunctions: ideational (field), interpersonal (tenor), and textual (mode).

Examining genre using an SFL approach to grammar does not gloss over form or syntax. Rather, "linguistic form is best viewed as functional in nature" (Painter, 1989, p. 20). Grammatical structures are constructed through the process of meaning making. Thus, they are not dichotomized. In this way, SFL is unique from other grammars as "rather than form preceding function, the two are seen as mutually dependent" (Painter, 1989, p. 21). Traditional grammars focus less on meaning making in text and primarily emphasize structure (Rose & Martin, 2012). In the U.S. context, SFL has been operationalized in schooling practices mostly through school–university partnerships, and research indicates teachers' use of SFL to inform literacy instruction with students supports robust pedagogical practices (see Achugar, Schleppegrell, & Oteiza, 2007; Brisk & Zisselsberger, 2011; Gebhard & Martin, 2011; Gebhard, Willett, Caicedo, & Piedra, 2011; Schleppegrell & Achugar, 2003). The forthcoming section describes the case study previously mentioned where elementary grade teachers, with support from a school–university partnership, used SFL to inform a genre-based approach to teaching writing.

Context of the study

In 2008, the Morrison Elementary School (a pseudonym) and a local private university began a three-year collaboration focused on improving writing pedagogy at the school. During the 2009–2010 academic year, the Morrison Elementary School (prekindergarten to fifth grade) had an enrollment of 386 students. The student population was 27.3% African American, 11.7% Asian, 54.5% Hispanic, 2.6% White, 0.3% Pacific Islander, and 3.4% Multi-racial (see Table 4.1).

Table 4.1. Morrison student demographics

Title	% of School	% of District	% of State
First language not English	62.1	38.8	15.6
Limited English proficient	43.6	20.4	6.2
Low-income	87.7	75.6	32.9
Special education	13.0	19.6	17.0

The partnership was led by María Estela Brisk, a professor in the field of bilingualism and literacy development. Her knowledge of literacy and expertise with English language learners (ELLs) directed the partnership in using a genre-based approach to the teaching of writing. This genre-based pedagogy was informed by SFL and designed and implemented by partnership stakeholders: Dr. Brisk, her doctoral students, of whom I was one, Morrison teachers (general and specialists), and the school principal. Knowledge about SFL, genre, and writing pedagogy were developed through ongoing professsional development (PD). The PD was constructed and administered by Dr. Brisk in conjunction with her doctoral students.

Teacher professional development

In the first year of the partnership (2008–2009), all third, fourth, fifth grade teachers, specialists (including art, physical education, computer, and science teachers), and the school principal attended a two-day summer writing institute held at the university. During the institute, participants learned the theory of SFL and the language demands of the genres commonly taught at the elementary school level: Recount, Narrative, Procedure, Report, Explanation, and Exposition. Teachers also collaboratively created annual writing calendars outlining which genres would be taught at each grade level and at what point during the school year they would be taught.

During the school year, teachers met weekly in grade-level planning groups and Dr. Brisk attended these planning sessions monthly. The meetings provided opportunities for teachers in small, grade-level groups to create genre-based lessons, construct student writing activities, and collaboratively evaluate student writing. During the first year of the partnership, teachers' classroom writing instruction was observed weekly by doctoral students from the university. All doctoral students had expertise in elementary literacy instruction. The observations and detailed field notes documented the writing instruction provided to students. These observations also functioned as a form of professional development as teachers and doctoral students collaborated about best instructional practices.

In the second year of the partnership (2009–2010), the teachers again attended a three-day summer writing institute at the university. During the third day of the summer institute, kindergarten, first, and second grade teachers from the elementary school came to the university and learned about SFL and genre-based pedagogy. The third, fourth, and fifth grade teachers, who had attended the institute during the previous summer and had implemented the genre-based pedagogy for one year, gave presentations about their work with students. Teachers shared what they had learned from the use of SFL to guide their practice and provided personal stories about teaching the genres of writing to students. During the second year of the partnership, all teachers in kindergarten, first, second, third, fourth, and fifth grades, in addition to science teachers, the principal, and specialists received ongoing professional development. This was the first year that the genre-based pedagogy was implemented school-wide and involved general education and Sheltered English Immersion (SEI) classes, which are special classes in the state specifically designed to provide English language support for new, arriving, non-native speakers.

The PD carried on in the third year of the partnership (2010–2011); doctoral students continued to visit classrooms at the Morrison across all grade levels on a weekly basis. They provided feedback to teachers on writing instruction, and Dr. Brisk continued to meet with grade-level teams monthly to analyze student work, further teachers' understanding of SFL, and share mentor texts with participants. Moreover, resources were provided to teachers across multiple years of the partnership. For example, teachers received a binder describing SFL and were given two books authored by Beverly Derewianka entitled, *Exploring How Texts Work* and *A Grammar Companion for Primary Teachers*. In addition, teachers acquired mentor texts in each taught genre. Overall, the partnership strived to enact changes in teachers' writing pedagogy using SFL through ongoing teacher PD.

Methodology

Observations of fourth and fifth grade teachers' writing instruction from the first to the third year of the partnership were analyzed using codes informed by SFL to answer the research question: *Does the content of the writing instruction in the fourth and fifth grades change in the areas of genre purpose, stage, language, and tenor during the three years of the partnership, if so, how?*

All observations of teachers' writing instruction in the fourth and fifth grades were conducted by doctoral students who were members of the university research team. Most of the doctoral students had previous elementary school teaching experience. During the partnership, the number of doctoral students performing observations in the fourth and fifth grades ranged from two to four.

A total of 97 observations were conducted (see Table 4.2) of ten teachers. Many of these teachers during the three years taught both fourth and fifth grade due to grade-level reassignment by the school principal. Teacher attrition led to the loss of three teachers from Year 2 to Year 3. Variation in the number of observations specifically from Year 1 to Year 2 can be attributed to the genre-based writing approach going school-wide in Year 2. Teachers began requiring more assistance across all grade levels, which limited the amount of time doctoral students had to observe in these grades.

Table 4.2. Observation by year, grade, and teacher

	Year 1		**Year 2**		**Year 3**	
Total # of observations	54		17		26	
Grade	4th	5th	4th	5th	4th	5th
# of Observations	13	41	9	8	9	17
# of Teachers	3	5	3	2	2	3

Observations were conducted weekly. They ranged in length of time, and on average were from 25 to 60 minutes. This variation occurred due to teaching style, scheduling, and other conflicts stemming from the schooling context. The primary purpose for the observations was to document the teachers' writing instruction. To capture this, observers recorded field notes. These notes documented employed teaching strategies, recorded how teachers verbalized writing content to students, documented teachers' writings on the whiteboards, reported students' responses in class, and described resources employed by the teachers, such as graphic organizers. In addition, writing posters created by the teachers between observations, which were located on the classroom walls to aid students, were transcribed.

Field notes were chosen rather than other data collection methods, such as audio and video recordings, in order to be less intrusive in the classroom. The intent was to capture the most authentic instruction in the classroom setting. Field note methods may collect less reliable data in that capturing verbatim teachers' instructional language with students is difficult compared with audio and video recordings, but the validity of these data may be greater than recordings, as teachers potentially feel more at ease being observed and therefore employ instruction similar to what they do when not being observed.

Findings

Analyses of the observation data indicated changes over three years occurred to the content of instruction focused on teaching genre. Instruction evolved regarding the teaching of purpose, stage, language, and tenor. Moreover, analyses indicated that teachers' use of metalanguage changed.

Metalanguage of genre

Metalanguage is defined in this chapter as language used when discussing language and aspects of genre, such as stages. The employed metalanguage came from SFL. Instruction noticeably transformed in the third year, and teachers began to commonly use metalanguage to discuss language and features of text. The use of metalanguage cut across most areas of content: discourse, language, and tenor. For instance, the word "genre" was used so frequently it became part of the lexicon of instruction in classes. Instruction mostly used metalanguage to reference aspects of stages associated with the genres. This precise language came about in posed questions to students, for example, "Who can recall what the thesis statement was?" and "Ok, what was their claim?" Similar metalanguage usage occurred in the first and second years to discuss aspects of stages, such as *claim*, *argument*, *reasons*, *resolution* and *orientation*. However, incidents involving this language were less frequent than in the third year. Across the classes, the metalanguage usage appeared to be contingent on the years in the partnership and increased accordingly.

During the initial years of the partnership, imprecise language was more commonly employed during instruction. For example, in the second year, when teaching the Persuasive genre, a teacher commented, "Now remember what you need to answer this prompt—details. Use your vocabulary and include details to describe your three reasons why this person is your favorite person." In this example, the instruction used imprecise language, *details*, to reference the stage feature "evidence." Another teacher in the same year during instruction stated, "Yes, you really need that one good main idea and then add lots of details to it." In this instance, the teacher used the lexicon of *details* to reference the stage feature of *reasons*.

In the third year, instruction further evolved and began to employ metalanguage to discuss language features. Primarily, the metalanguage was used to teach *adjectives*. For instance, a teacher commented, "These are all words that describe. All words that we call adjectives." Despite some examples, instruction only rarely employed metalanguage to reference language features and instead continued to employ vague language to identify these features.

Purpose of genre

In the third year of the partnership, teachers' genre-based instruction focused on educating students about various written purposes. This instruction took the form of teaching students about one specific genre for approximately four to six weeks and then transitioning to a new genre study. Overall, despite instruction that reviewed different genres, the content expressed across the targeted genres emphasized similar aspects of discourse. For instance, instruction commonly involved teachers using SFL terminology to explicitly name the genres being studied, such as Persuasive, Historical Recount, or Fictional Narrative and then providing students with the purposes of the genres. This focus existed throughout the partnership, but a greater emphasis was placed on teaching the purposes of the genres in the third year. For example, in the third year, when learning the Persuasive genre, a teacher commented to students, "If you are writing in a Persuasive genre, it is your job to convince." Another teacher in the same year when teaching the Report genre stated to students, "Remember the purpose for the author is to inform."

This increased focus on the purposes of the genres often occurred in conjunction with other teaching. For example, in Table 4.3, a teacher instructed students about the use of *word webs*. During the instruction, the teacher deviated from the content about word webs to reinforce the purpose of Report writing: *to inform*. In previous years, these types of incidents rarely occurred. Initially, the instruction primarily taught the purposes of the genres only when the genres were first introduced to students and then were seldom reinforced during the genre units.

Table 4.3. Conversation between a teacher and students regarding genre purpose

Teacher	We are now going to look at [student's name] piece. Notice how on the corners of the poster she provided some bulleted information. What was [student's name] purpose in using the word web?
Student (1)	I think it was to inform.
Teacher	Remember the purpose for the author is to inform. What should the reader come away with when reading you posters?
Student (2)	You should know more about snakes.
Teacher	Even if they do not want to learn about snakes, your job is to get them to learn more so you have to be creative.

In addition to the increased emphasis on the purposes of the genres, the instruction in the third year began to use more robust language to better define the genre purposes. This richer language emerged when explaining the purpose of the persuasive genre. In previous years, the instruction frequently stated the purpose of the Persuasive genre as to "persuade" or "convince" and rarely elaborated. In comparison, the instruction in the third year began to give better explanations of the purposes. Specifically, in regards to the genre of Persuasive, the instruction started to contain synonyms for "persuade" or "convince." For example, a teacher wrote synonyms of persuade and convince on the board for students, which included: "argue, induce, lead on, get, talk into, win over." These synonyms, developed from discussions about the purpose of the genre, likely provided students with a better understanding of the purpose of the targeted genre. In summary, instruction changed regarding the teaching of genre over time and became more explicit.

Staging of genre

During the partnership, instruction evolved regarding the stages of the genres and specifically their features in text. The features teachers taught the students composed the stages of the introduction and body of the genres. The features that make up the stages of the conclusion of the genres were seldom taught, and this instruction remained unchanged during the partnership. This likely occurred due to the PD not emphasizing this stage, because of limited PD time. Regardless of this lack of change, instruction transformed involving the features of the other stages and a greater amount of time was dedicated to teaching these to students. Also, the quality of the content about these features improved and led to richer instruction.

In the third year, the instruction routinely discussed the stage features of the genres. For instance, when teaching the Persuasive genre, the instruction reviewed the features of *thesis statement* or *claim*, *reasons*, and *evidence* and examined texts in order to identify the features. Moreover, the instruction included explanations of the features' functions in text. For example, Table 4.4 displays a fourth grade teacher's instruction with students.

Table 4.4. Conversation between a teacher and students about stage features

Teacher	What did you notice in the first paragraph compared to the other ones? Did the author have a plan?
Student (1)	It was clear the author had a plan because all the reasons were in the first paragraph in order.
Teacher	So in the first paragraph all of the reasons for the argument were there, so I hope you noticed after the first paragraph each paragraph, like the second one here, contained a reason with evidence to support the reason. In the first paragraph, what was in it?
Student (1)	The reasons and the statement.
Teacher	What kind of statement?
Student (1)	Thesis statement.
Teacher	Ok, so notice the introduction had the thesis statement and reasons for this piece. So do you think the author had a plan before starting to write?
Student (2)	Yes!

Instruction in the first and second years reviewed the stage features within the taught genres. However, the content of the instruction for most teachers was unclear and often incorrect. The reason for this ambiguous instruction came about from the use of imprecise language or wrong terminology to define the features. For instance, in the first year, a teacher stated, "What is the other big argument, reason?" Similarly, in the second year, a teacher commented, "So our intros have three things that need to happen. They state our reason, give our three reasons, and grab your attention." These examples illustrate how incorrect lexicon was initially used.

During these years, instruction that used incorrect metalanguage to reference the stage features may have stemmed from the teachers' lack of understanding them and their functions in text. For example, in the first year of the partnership, instruction routinely referred to "thesis statement" as an "introduction" or "topic sentence" and used this lexicon interchangeably. It is important to note to students that an introduction does contain a thesis statement, but a thesis statement does not constitute an introduction. Furthermore, a thesis statement is not a topic sentence and they serve different functions in text: A topic sentence introduces the topic of a paragraph and functions to foster text cohesion, while a thesis statement functions to state the claim or position of the author in the text. In comparison, instruction in the third year consistently employed precise language when referencing stage features and provided accurate explanations of the features and their functions in text.

In the third year, instruction further evolved and began discussing the interconnectedness of the stage features. For example, a teacher commented to students, "Does [student's name] evidence support her reason? Does her argument match her reasons?" The instruction focused on the connection between the features of "argument" and "reasons" and between the features of *reasons* and *evidence*. These stage features collectively function to develop text cohesion and to foster discourse meaning. This change was significant as prior instruction taught them in isolation of one another. Overall, this change in instruction may have occurred due to teachers possessing a better understanding of SFL and specifically the way in which the stages function in text to unfold meaning.

Language use in genre

Changes occurred to the content of instruction in regards to language during the partnership; however, the instruction about language was very limited. Moreover, the quality of the instruction that did occur varied among the teachers. The changes included more effective use of writing activities to teach language and better reinforcement of previously taught language features during the genre-based writing instruction. In addition, instruction began educating students about the functions of the language features in text and their role in achieving the purpose of the taught genres. For example, in Table 4.5, a teacher explained possessive nouns by providing an example, naming the language feature, and providing an explanation of its function. This instruction provided students with an understanding of the role possessive nouns serve in text. In comparison, instruction in the first and second years seldom emphasized the functions of the language features in text. Rather, the instruction about the language features lacked depth and connection with their purposes in text.

Table 4.5. Discussing the function of language features in text

Teacher	[Reads the sentence aloud: "The boy looked into my father's eyes."] What do you notice in that sentence? What do you suppose that apostrophe is about?
Student	To show what that boy is doing to that father or like [pause], kinda what the father owns.
Teacher	We put an apostrophe to show ownership—my father's eyes. A singular possessive noun shows one person's possession whereas plural means more than one. To make a singular noun show possession you add an apostrophe s like I did here [pointing to the board].

Instruction in the third year also changed and made connections between the functions of the taught language features with the purposes of the genres.

This instruction illustrated how language usage functions to achieve the purposes of the genres. It is important to note that this instruction happened infrequently and did not occur with all teachers.

Instruction focused on the functions of the language features and the purposes of the genres most often occurred through examinations of text. For example, in Table 4.6, a teacher, in conjunction with students, analyzed the language used in a persuasive text. This text persuaded readers that staying at home to watch a movie is better than going to the movie theater. This text was used during the teacher PD to illustrate how language functions to achieve the purpose of the genre.

Table 4.6. Conversation between a teacher and students examining text

Teacher	Can you tell us what the title of this piece is?
All Students	The Hazards of Movie Going.
Teacher	So what do you think this piece is about? What is another word we can use for hazard? Before we look at the thesis statement let's first read the text again and listen for the language used to make the author's point. [text is reread] So what are some strong words that the author uses to make his point?
Student (1)	Comfort of my own living room.
Teacher	So "comfort." What other language was used?
Student (2)	Shouting at the screen and running around the aisles.
Teacher	Notice he [referring to the author] did not just say kids running. He is telling the reader exactly what happens when he is at the movies. What else?
Student (3)	Thirty-five minute drive down a congested highway.
Teacher	Right! He did not just say the highway. He said the "congested" highway… So what other language was used?
Student (5)	I usually have to wait in a long line at the concession booth.
Teacher	Yes. What else?
Student (6)	A musty smell
Teacher	Yeah! Not just a smell, but a musty smell ... So not only did the author carefully craft his argument with a good thesis and reasons with evidence, he was also careful with the language he used. On that note, I would like you to think about the type of language you used on your turkey piece. I want you to go into our writer's notebook and add some extremely descriptive language to your turkey piece. I want you to look at the piece you planned and wrote in paragraph form and now **think about the type of language this author used to help you see his argument in your mind.**

The example shows how instruction linked language use and function in achieving the purpose of the genre (see bolded text). In comparison, instruction in the first and second years did not explicitly link the taught language features and their functions in achieving the genres' purposes.

Tenor in genre

Analyses showed changes occurred over time to the content of the genre-based writing instruction in regards to tenor. In the third year of the partnership, instruction began to call attention to tenor. Teachers did not use the term *tenor* with students. Rather, they commonly referenced the relationship between the writer and audience or "voice" in text. This newfound focus on tenor was operationalized in the form of having students write for many audiences. The audiences included peers, students in different grades, the school district superintendent, school principal, and teachers within the school. Instruction in previous years did not require students to write for different audiences. Instead, instruction most often had students write for their classroom teacher or it never explicitly named the audience.

In comparison, instruction in the third year frequently referenced audience. For example, a teacher commented to students, "Remember before you can make a commercial, you have to know your audience in order to persuade them." Another teacher clearly stated the audience to the students, "You have to persuade other fifth graders, that is your audience …" Instruction in the first and second years lacked this emphasis on tenor. When it was taught, instruction primarily made the connection between audience and content. For example, when discussing a student's Historical Report about Patriots during the American Revolution, a teacher commented, "If I was a third or a fourth grader, I would wonder what you meant that people were in your house." This statement referenced how Patriots occupied peoples' residences for military purposes. The example captures how the teacher's instruction focused on the importance of an author considering their audience's background knowledge about a topic when writing. Similar instruction that linked audience and content was found even more in the third year of the partnership.

In the third year, the instruction about tenor evolved and started to focus on how audience affects language use in text. It is important to note that most of this instruction did not explicitly name this connection. Rather, the instruction tended to provide scenarios for students in which they had to employ their understanding of appropriate oral language usage given a context. For instance, in Table 4.7, a teacher provides a scenario to students that involves them speaking with the state governor.

Table 4.7. Conversation between a teacher and students focused on context

Teacher	Who governs the entire state?
Student 1	Obama
Student 2	Is it that black dude that just won?
Teacher	Let's all say Deval Patrick.

Students	Deval Patrick
Teacher	What would we say to Deval Patrick? Would we say, "hey, the black dude who just won?" Is that what it would sound like?
Students	No! [laughing]
Student 3	It would say, "dear and his name, please ... "
Teacher	Okay, so your language is much more polite.

In this example, the students identified the appropriate type of oral language to use when speaking with the governor, and this comprehension was expected to transfer to students' writing. The instruction gave students some understanding of how audience affects language.

In addition, instruction began to emphasize audience when teaching language features, such as vocabulary. Students' comments suggest they were developing an understanding of this connection. For instance, when discussing a report about volcanoes written for second graders, a student commented, "I told them about the volcanoes when they erupt. I gave them some vocabulary words they might not know." In this case, the student recognized that the audience, second graders, may not have the background knowledge to understand some of the vocabulary in the text and provided brief definitions of key words associated with the topic. Overall, instructional changes occurred about tenor during the partnership. These changes included an increased emphasis on teaching about audience and its influences on text, having students write for an array of authentic audiences, highlighting the connection between audience and content, and beginning to teach the link between audience and language use.

Discussion

The study findings showed that initial changes to the content of instruction stemmed from the use of metalanguage in the teaching of genre (purpose and staging) and tenor. The PD focused on these topics because they aligned with what teachers, in some capacity, were already doing at the Morrison. Using SFL, the PD further expanded this knowledge, which transferred into the teachers' genre-based pedagogy in the classroom. Changes to the content of instruction involving the teaching of language began to occur in the third year, but mostly remained limited. One reason for this may be that the PD mostly emphasized genre and focused less on language. However, the development began to have more of an emphasis on language in the third year. Another reason that explicit teaching of language was limited may be that language instruction took longer to enact than other content because the PD did not sufficiently develop teachers' knowledge about language. The teachers may have needed almost three years of development in order to foster a competent level of understanding regarding how language functions to make meaning in text.

These findings indicated that the process of operationalizing SFL in a genre-based approach to the teaching of writing takes a tremendous amount of time, and, even with three years of exposure, some aspects are still not adopted. In fact, teachers only began making significant changes to the content of instruction after receiving ongoing SFL-informed PD for two years. One reason that may explain why teachers took so long to enact significant changes to their instruction is because they were in what Fullan (2001) defined as the *implementation dip.* The implementation dip is when performance and confidence decrease during a period attempting something new. Fullan explained that people in the implementation dip are "experiencing two kinds of problems when they are in the dip—the social-psychological fear of change, and the lack of technical know-how or skills to make the change work" (p. 41).

In the first year of exposure to SFL, teachers may have experienced anxiety and unease about using a linguistic theory to inform practice. The difficulty of operationalizing theory in practice and making changes to writing instruction may have caused concern. Furthermore, the teachers had very limited knowledge about SFL and genre in comparison with their understanding in the second year and beyond, which also likely contributed to the lack of change identified in the first year. The implementation dip cannot be overlooked in endeavors where teachers are using SFL to inform genre-based pedagogy. This aspect of the change process takes time, and ongoing assistance is needed for teachers in the form of content and emotional support in order to enact desired pedagogical reform.

In conclusion, the findings showed that over time SFL can foster teachers' understanding of genre—specifically how language is used to make meaning. Teachers' knowledge transfers via their genre-based pedagogy with students. Regardless of specific context, teacher educators and reformers must be aware that the processes of learning SFL and using it to teach genre and language take an extensive amount of time. However, the benefits to the quality of writing instruction may exceed those of quicker approaches to change.

References

Achugar, M., Schleppegrell, M., & Oteiza, T. (2007). Engaging teachers in language analysis: A functional linguistic approach to reflective literacy. *English Teaching: Practice and Critique, 6*(2), 8–24.

Brisk, M. E., & Zisselsberger, M. (2011). We've let them in on the secret: Using SFL theory to improve the teacher of writing to bilingual learners. In T. Lucas (Ed.), *Teacher preparation for linguistically diverse classrooms: A resource for teacher educators* (pp. 111–126). New York: Routledge.

Butt, D., Fahey, R., Feez, S., Spinks, S., & Yallop, C. (2000). *Using functional grammar: An explorer's guide*. Sydney: National Centre for English Language Teaching and Research.

Cutler, L., & Graham, S. (2008). Primary grade instruction: A national survey. *Journal of Educational Psychology, 100*(4), 907–919. http://dx.doi.org/10.1037/a0012656

Eggins, S. (1994). *An introduction to systemic functional linguistics*. London: Pinter Publishers.

Fullan, M. (2001). *Leading in a culture of change*. San Francisco: Jossey-Bass.

Gebhard, M., & Martin, J. R. (2011). Grammar and literacy learning. In D. Lapp & D. Fisher (Eds.), *Handbook of research on teaching the English language arts* (3rd ed.) (pp. 297–304). New York: Routledge.

Gebhard, M., Willett, J., Caicedo, J. P. J., & Piedra, A. (2011). Systemic functional linguistics, teachers' professional development, and ELLs' academic literacy practices. In T. Lucas (Ed.), *Teacher preparation for linguistically diverse classrooms: A resource for teacher educators* (pp. 91–110). New York: Routledge.

Gilbert, J., & Graham, S. (2010). Teaching writing to elementary students in grades 4–6: A national survey. *The Elementary School Journal, 110*(4), 494–518. http://dx.doi.org/10.1086/651193

Graham, S., & Harris R. K. (2013). Designing an effective writing program. In S. Graham, C. A. MacArthur & J. Fitzgerald (Eds.), *Best practices in writing instruction* (2nd ed.) (pp. 3–25). New York: The Guilford Press.

Halliday, M. A. K. (1994). *An introduction to functional grammar*. New York: Routledge, Chapman and Hall.

Halliday, M. A. K., & Hasan, R. (1989). *Language, context, and text: Aspects of language in a social-semiotic perspective*. Oxford: Oxford University Press.

Hinkel, E. (2002). *Second language writers' text*. Mahwah, NJ: Lawrence Erlbaum Associates.

National Center for Education Statistics. (2012). *Writing in 2011: National assessment of educational progress at grades 8 and 12* (NCES Publication No. 2012-470). Washington, DC: U.S. Government Printing Office.

National Commission on Writing. (2003). *The neglected R: The need for a writing revolution*. Retrieved June 10, 2014, from www.collegeboard.com

Painter, C. (1989). Learning language: A functional view of language development. In R. Hasan & J. R. Martin (Eds.), *Language development: Learning language, learning culture: Meaning and choice in language: Studies for Michael Halliday* (pp. 18–65). Norwood, NJ: Ablex Publishing Corporation.

Rose, D., & Martin, J. R. (2012). *Learning to write, reading to learn: Genre knowledge and pedagogy in the Sydney School*. Bristol, CT: Equinox Publishing.

Schleppegrell, M. J., & Achugar, M. (2003). Learning language and learning history: A functional linguistics approach. *TESOL Journal, 12*(2), 21–27.

5 Genre-based principles in a content-based English as a second language pull-out classroom

J. Andrés Ramírez

Introduction

The education and academic achievement of all students, including English language learners (ELLs) is "nested" within particular sociocultural conditions (Weis, 1988). Given the persistent achievement gap of ELLs as compared to their native English-speaking counterparts (Short & Fitzsimmons, 2007), their disproportionally higher dropout rates (Kim, 2011), disproportional representation in special education (Artiles, Klingner, Sullivan, & Firerros, 2010), and dissonance between what research says about how to better educate these students and the policies that are implemented (García & Kleifgen, 2010; Gutiérrez & Jaramillo, 2006), it is clear that the education of these students is especially filled with contradictions, charged debates and failed attempts to provide them with the school and non-school conditions they need and deserve to succeed.

One of the major contradictions that will be explored in this chapter is the prevalence of the English as a second language (ESL) pull-out approach in the United States (Crawford & Educational Resources Information Center (U.S.), 1997; García & Baetens Beardsmore, 2009) and its dissociation with disciplinary knowledge despite the fact that ESL taught via content area instruction (social studies, math, science, and so on) is associated with higher long-term educational attainment (Snow, Met, & Genesee, 1989; Thomas & Collier, 1997). In ESL pull-out programs, students are taken out of their regular classrooms (usually daily for one to two periods of instruction) and given one-on-one or small group instruction in English, which is usually unrelated to the content area instruction they receive while in their mainstream classrooms.

This chapter describes the genre-based procedures and pedagogy of engagement principles inherent to the Strategic Alignment approach (Ramirez, 2008) that enriched ELLs' academic literacy ontogenesis (Rose & Martin, 2012), as this approach not only prevented ELLs from missing the science content they were not getting at the time of ESL pull-out instruction but focused on scaffolding the genre of Explanation, a prominent but taken for granted genre in science, in the context of a content-based learning expedition on the life cycle of Atlantic salmon in the Connecticut river. The chapter demonstrates how systemic functional linguistics and its associated genre-based methodology can be used successfully so that ESL students with developmental needs in English can also attain high levels of discipline-specific academic literacy even when pull-out is the prevalent way students receive ESL services.

Review of the literature

As is also the case around the world (Luke, 1996), literacy education in the U.S.A. has been a hotly contested issue for decades (Baker, 2010; Rodby, 1992). During this time, the pendulum that has been literacy reform and educational reform has swung dramatically from one extreme to the other and back many times (Baker, 2010). With the meta-analysis of research conducted by the National Reading Panel in 2000, the now familiar either/or debate came back stronger than ever (see, for example, Allington, 2002).

The harsh debate that has followed (see, for example, Eldesky & Bomer, 2005) resulted (as it did in the late 1960s) in debates focused on early reading that ended up silencing reading issues beyond grade 3 or 4, the development of academic literacy, and reading across the curriculum. As the United States entered what progressives have rightly called a "high stakes education era" (Lipman, 2004) exacerbated by unprecedented federal mandates, proponents of meaning-emphasis approaches and even those whose expertise is in ELLs got caught up in the debate and slipped into careless attention to the particularity and importance of explicitly attending to the ontogenesis of academic literacy for ELLs and to the specialized nature of building disciplinary knowledge. For example, Krashen strongly favors a theory of involuntary acquisition of nearly all the so-called "language skills" through sustained silent reading (SSR) or voluntary reading. By simply reading, students will become better readers, acquire a large vocabulary, have better grammatical competence, and become better spellers among other advantages (Krashen, 2004). Along the same lines, with regards to Whole Language, perhaps the most recognized of the meaning-emphasis approaches, Carlos Ovando, Virginia Collier, and Carole Combs, write: "Whole language emphasizes a focus on meaning first and *the parts come naturally later*, as students are ready to focus on the details of language, through reading authentic texts and the students' own writing" (Ovando, Collier, & Combs, 2003 [my emphasis]). As such, this debate has contributed to obscure and weakening disciplinary knowledge as an object of study, certainly emergent from but irreducible to how individuals know or how knowledge reflects social power (Maton, 2013).

In her critique of progressivist and later constructivist notions of inquiry learning, Christie (2004) points out that constructivist meaning-based pedagogies take language for granted and emphasize the benefits of self-expression that undermines and weakens the discipline base of school subjects, confuses the goals of education, and compromises the role of teacher authority. This weakening is perhaps nowhere as evident in the United States as in the lack of explicit attention to the "language of schooling" (Schleppegrell, 2004) essential to build necessary disciplinary knowledge, a needed focus that has been eclipsed by the already mentioned debates and the resulting generalized attention to literacy strategies and self-expression with dire consequences to all students, but especially to language minority ones (Delpit, 1995, 2012; Moje & Speyer, 2008). Christie, along with other scholars of the so called "Sydney School," have promoted a genre-based pedagogy which enabled the identification of the genres every student should learn to write in primary school and set out to develop a pedagogy and curriculum to make sure they learn them (Martin & Rose, 2008).

Perhaps one of the of the most fruitful, promising, and sound attempts to overcome this so called "knowledge-blindness" in which knowledge as an object is obscured in educational research (Maton, 2013) has been the recent but already robust collaboration of social realism and SFL (Christie & Maton, 2011). Colloquially referred to as "elevator talk" by educational linguists associated with SFL and technically defined as "cumulative modality" by Legitimation Code Theory (LCT) (Maton, 2011), this approach highlights the crucial role of principled talk-around text for knowledge-building attributes of disciplinary knowledge. According to Maton, who explores the basis of cumulative disciplinary knowledge building, varying the relative strengths of semantic gravity (represented as +/− SG) and semantic density (represented as +/−SD) generates four principal semantic codes of legitimation that can be purposefully enacted in the classroom in the form of a principled talk-around text (Maton, 2011).

Maton (2013) explains that, because all meanings relate to a context of some kind, semantic gravity (SG) conceptualizes how much they depend on that context. Relative to the degree to which they depend on context or not, SG may be relatively stronger (+) or weaker (−) along a continuum of strengths where the stronger the SG (SG+), the more meaning is dependent on its context, the weaker the SG (SG−), the less dependent meaning is on its context. Semantic density (SD) refers to the degree of condensation of meaning within a broad spectrum of sociocultural practices ranging from symbols to expressions, gestures, or even clothing. As with SG, SD may be relatively stronger (+) or weaker (−) along a continuum of strengths. The stronger the SD (SD+), the more meanings are condensed within practices; the weaker the SD (SD−), the less meanings are condensed. Notably, when these semantic continua include change over time in the context of principled talk-around-text, the model comes alive as the analysis of any piece of discourse can focus on the moving up and down the semantic continua with instances of, for example, the weakening (SG↓) or strengthening SG (SG↑). The latter (SG↑) can be seen as pedagogical discourse moves from the concrete particulars of a specific case towards generalizations and abstractions, the former (SG↓) as pedagogical discourse moves from abstract or generalized ideas towards concrete and delimited cases. A proposed pedagogical framework in which movement across the semantic continua figured prominently to align strategically with the nested conditions particular to this specific context is explained next.

Critical pedagogy as Strategic Alignment

Certainly, critical pedagogy has come to mean very different things for different people (Giroux, 2001; Luke, 1996; Shor & Pari, 1999). Strategic Alignment serves as a critical pedagogic framework that regulates and aligns the kind of official or non-official knowledge a teacher chooses to foreground and when (Ramirez, 2008). Such regulation necessarily involves a complex interaction between societal reservoirs and individual repertoires or between what Bernstein (2000) calls the ORF (official recontextualizing field) and the PRF (pedagogic recontextualizing field) in which the teacher figures prominently, as s/he as an adult agent of semiotic meditation is no longer culturally neutral and generic but represents and is the voice of a distinct ideology (Hasan, 1999). The ORF is a pedagogic reservoir representing the "voice" of ideas; that is, the limits on what could potentially be realized or said legitimately within a pedagogic relation. On the other hand, PRF represents the "message" of ideas; that is, the contextual realization or what is actually said—the message, which, although depends on what could be said (voice), cannot be determined. In the specific case of the school that is the focus of the analysis in the following part of this chapter, the "mandated" instruction that will be described in the next section (expeditionary learning, ESL pull-out model, Fast ForWord) represents the official "voice" of ideas prescribed for this specific "nested community". The teacher's own pedagogic repertoire, the knowledge actually realized and foregrounded in the classroom, represents the actual "message."

As will be illustrated in the context of the focus school and classroom, Strategic Alignment is a highly dynamic, responsive, and contextual reservoir of pedagogical meaning potential that opens up "voice" or what could be said beyond the frame of narrow high stakes accountability as it simultaneously responds to a) standards and mandates, b) students' needs, rights, and backgrounds (including linguistic backgrounds, and c) thought collectives of the discipline (see Figure 5.1). Without attempting to exhaust all the potential of this model, this chapter highlights teaching that aligned to the students' needs, rights, and backgrounds aspects of the model through the focused tools of SFL theory and genre-based pedagogy "thought collectives" (Ramanathan, 2002). To purposefully and responsively apprentice ELLs to the value of actively participating in disciplinary discourse became both an imperative and a possibility within the Strategic Alignment framework as it played out in the specific context described here. Ingrained in the framework as implemented in this context was the importance of utilizing self-expression and activation of relevant background knowledge through developmentally appropriate linguistic strategies that followed the main genre-based principle of "guidance through interaction in the context of shared experience" (Rose & Martin, 2012, p. 58). This main principle served as an entry point into cumulative disciplinary knowledge building as a means to emphasize the importance of shared experience (including knowledge of genre writing), an important condition for successfully negotiating field (Rose & Martin, 2012, p. 65). Thus, and even though disciplinary knowledge played an essential role in pedagogical relations as it represents the accumulated disciplinary collective thought to be "recontexutalized" (in Bernstein's sense) in teaching, the approach accounts for the danger of trying to overcome the already described "knowledge-blindness" without succumbing into "knower-blindness" (Maton, 2013).

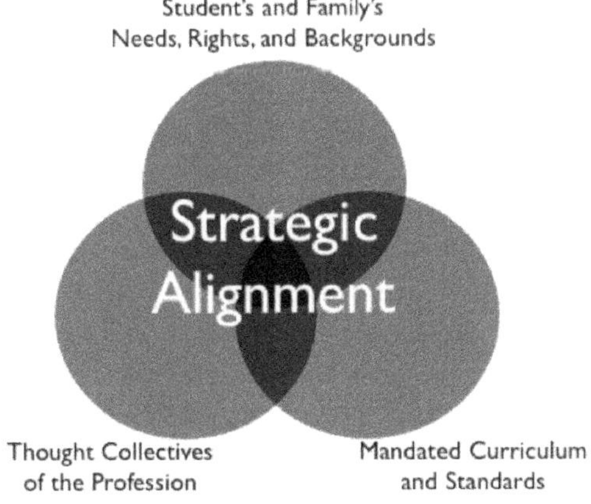

Figure 5.1. Strategic alignment

Context of the study

Teaching ESL at Pleasant Valley Middle School

As is the case in many parts of the United States, cities and schools have experienced radical demographic changes in the last part of the twentieth century. The percentage of Hispanics (41.0%) and Whites (17.9%) in the middle school that is the focus of this analysis corresponds to the growing number of Hispanics and decline in White population in the city where the school was located. The dismal achievement gaps of the city schools in general and of Pleasant Valley Middle School in particular led the school district to apply to the U.S. Department of Education Magnet Schools Assistance Program. To date, the program's main goal has been to increase diversity and assist in the desegregation of public schools and through unique educational programming designed to attract families to make an active choice to enroll children in such schools (Magnet School Assistance, n.d.).

Once the district was awarded with these funds, Pleasant Valley, along with nine others in the city, became "Expeditionary Learning" magnet schools. The school-wide model of Expeditionary Learning hoped to address academic subjects through challenging, standards-based units with hands-on projects that are often interdisciplinary in nature. Pleasant Valley Middle School prides itself in having students participate in "Learning Expeditions" in which they conduct first-hand research in important topics in science and social studies.

Fast ForWord: an unnecessary extra layer of remediation

As a complement to the ESL pull-out instruction already mentioned, another remedial literacy intervention called Fast ForWord was mandated in the school. Fast ForWord (used in the U.S.A., Australia, and the U.K.) is a collection of computer-based language intervention programs aimed specifically at children aged 4 to 14, seeking to improve the skills of children who have language learning difficulties and target their reading and oral language skills through themed games and interactive activities. Fast ForWord proponents claim that it is "based on over 30 years of neuroscience research" and that it has produced significant gains in reading achievement. Studies cited, however, are based on a number of privately conducted, in-house studies without randomized controlled trials, no control groups and with no evidence of controlling for other variables affecting results (Strong, Torgerson, Torgerson, & Hulme, 2011). In fact, a recent metastudy of sound methodological studies found that the program had no significant effects on children's single-word reading skills, passage-reading comprehension, receptive language, and expressive language. In fact, four of the effect sizes found by the team were negative, indicating that children who received Fast ForWord did worse compared to controls or other treatments (Strong et al., 2011).

Method

Participants

The ESL class met six times a week, with three of these hours dedicated to regular ESL intervention and the other three hours to the Fast ForWord program. This particular class was made up of a combination of seventh and eighth graders and was composed of eight students in total (six girls and two boys) in which I was the teacher. Six students were from Puerto Rico and the other two from Ethiopia. Because the great majority of ELLs in the nation and in this school are Hispanics, a somewhat detailed profile on one of these students follows.

Jorge: ELL with special needs

During my time teaching at Pleasant Valley Middle School, Jorge was perhaps my most vulnerable student. As was the case of more than 80% of the total Hispanic population in the city, Jorge was born in Puerto Rico. He was in eighth grade in a self-included special education classroom with other students with mild disabilities. This bright, respectful, and fun 13-year old had been diagnosed with Attention Deficit Hyperactivity Disorder (ADHD) and used to take psychostimulants every day in the mornings. Despite this, Jorge presented himself as a happy young adolescent with great hopes for the future and unparalleled willingness and interest in learning.

Strategic alignment in the classroom

The focus and strength of genre-based pedagogy is the ontogenesis of academic identities. In other words, its basic pedagogical principles seek to lead students into "unpacking" the esoteric and elusive textual reservoir in which disciplinary knowledge in the academy is produced, appropriated, and distributed. However, successful apprenticeship and even credentialed mastery of disciplinary genres rarely is, in and by itself, sufficient. Following Allan Luke's call for genre pedagogy to be mindful of the denaturalizing and demystifying cultural texts by making explicit their codes while at the same time running the risk of failing to "situate, critique, interrogate, and transform these texts, their discourses and their institutional sites" (Luke, 1996), Strategic Alignment, understood as a critical pedagogy of engagement is necessary. This is so because without challenging the institutional discourses ingrained in the school's district treatment of ESL, the kind of instruction students would have received would be framed under traditional discourses and structures of remediation and compensatory education prevalent in ESL classes. A case in point that illustrates such differential structures (ORF in Bernstein's theory) is described below.

While Pleasant Valley teachers in core areas (English language arts, science, math, and social studies) met in teams by grade level for weekly planning, ESL teachers would meet with one another. This indeed promoted and favored a seriously compromised approach in which second language learning and academic learning were not integrated, jeopardizing student's rights to be apprenticed into disciplinary knowledge. After voicing this danger with the administration and my fellow eighth grade colleagues, I began attending the team meetings to participate in planning of learning expeditions and strategically align instruction to the needs, rights, and backgrounds of students. Now as a full participant in curriculum making, our common planning led us to focus on a science learning expedition to explore the life cycle of the Atlantic salmon to highlight an important concept in eighth grade science: the interconnectivity among biological systems. The expedition was called "Think Globally, Act Locally" and had as central content the study of Atlantic salmon in this eastern part of the country. As part of the expedition, the science classroom had a fish tank with salmon eggs. Students were able to witness first-hand the cycle of the salmon as the eggs later became sac fry. When sac fry evolved into fry, they were released into the Connecticut River by students accompanied by the team of teachers.

To align to and expand students' background knowledge (including genre writing knowledge) on this particular life cycle—what Rose and Martin (2012) call negotiating field to emphasize the importance of shared experience of the subject matter—I created a curricular macrogenre (Christie, 2002) for my own ESL pull-out classroom whose enduring understanding was: "Humans and other biological systems are interconnected in complex ways" (see Figure 5.2). To align to already established principles belonging to teaching ELL thought collectives and thus avoiding the problem of ELL students doing "double the work" (Short & Fitzsimmons, 2007), which refers to mastering unfamiliar academic content while still learning English, familiar cycles in nature—water cycle, seed growth cycle, photosynthesis, and the rock cycle—were used as content scaffolds in this curricular unit for the life cycle of the Atlantic salmon. Students' familiarity with these cycles not only promoted instruction that focused more on academic control of the focus Explanation genre, but it facilitated guidance through unfolding dialogue in the context of shared experience.

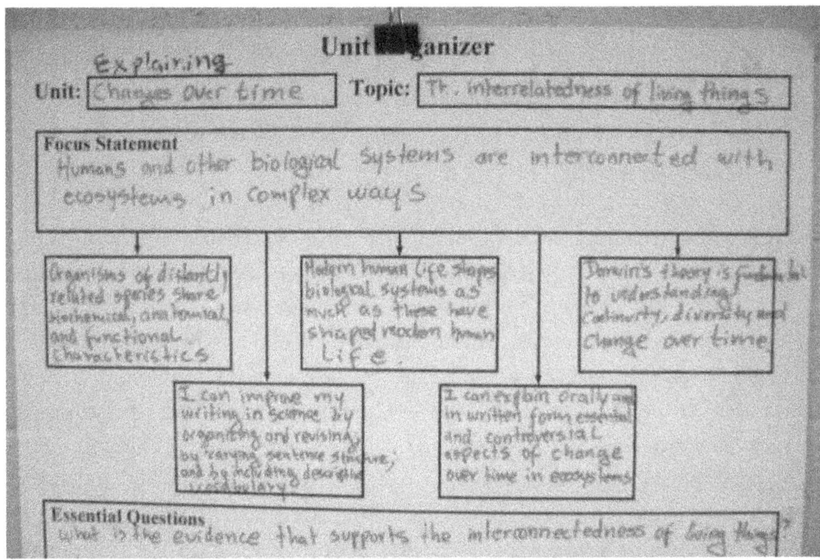

Figure 5.2. Explaining Changes Over Time curricular macrogenre

In the rest of this chapter, a description of the nature of the pedagogic dialogue that took place in the classroom is presented. The semantic codes already described, semantic gravity and semantic density along a continuum of weaker or stronger strengths, are utilized as a heuristic to illustrate how the process of packing and unpacking disciplinary knowledge played out in classroom dialogue. These codes seek to highlight the purposeful use of pedagogic discourse in the context of shared experience in this ESL classroom. As already detailed, weaker (−) or stronger (+) SG refers to the degree of connection to the context, and weaker (−) or stronger (+) SD refers to how condensed a term or concept is respectively.

Apprenticing students into disciplinary knowledge: unpacking discourse

One of the most useful tools (although general and elusive) that teachers working in all ESL models can utilize with students who have special needs is the Individualized Education Plan-Special Education (IEP). In Jorge's case, apart from his ADHD diagnosis that took center stage in his report, and a recommendation for teachers to "provide graphic organizers, charts, timelines; and shorten assignments," a list of academic goals for his writing development served as a starting point.

- At the end of this IEP period, he will demonstrate at least 6–12 months progress in writing skills. He will write with a clear focus, coherent organization, and sufficient detail.

- Write organized paragraphs with at least three supporting details and a conclusion in all subject areas with 80% accuracy in regards to spelling and grammar.

With no curriculum, lack of discipline base for school subjects, vague directives like "organized paragraphs" or "sufficient detail," and no mention of the genres to focus on, building Jorge's science subject knowledge and control over linguistic tools to "talking science" (Lemke, 1990) became a goal compatible with the overall goals of the already mentioned learning expedition and with the thought collectives evoked by Lemke. After analyzing the science standards to better align instruction, it became apparent that one of the most prominent genres, and therefore one that was important for students to have control over, was the Explanation genre. Specifically, science standards spell out scientific academic themes and concepts but take for granted the language to write successful explanations. More surprisingly, after turning to the state curriculum standards for English language arts for some direction on the Explanation, passing references to this genre were buried in general standards such as "connecting what has been read (plot/ideas/concepts) to prior knowledge, other texts, or the broader world of ideas, by referring to and explaining relevant ideas or themes."

Carrying on with the goal of all students becoming active participants in the disciplinary discourse of scientific explanations presupposed an explicit and well-informed stance on how Explanations are constructed and how they can be taught to students. Embracing the genre-based principle of treating language as a patterned resource for meaning-making through a meaningfully redundant pedagogy that was maximally supportive initially and allowed for gradual release of responsibility onto the student through purposeful talk-around texts (Macken-Horarik, Adoniou, de Oliveira, & Ramirez, 2011) was key. Also key was following the curriculum cycle of genre-based pedagogy (Derewianka, 2000; Rothery, 1996), in order to build the field by familiarizing students with life cycles and with the genre of Explanations. At this stage, and aligning to students' backgrounds, explanations and texts in the students' native languages were highly useful (+SG/−SD). Using a simple diagram of the water cycle projected onto a white board, students were prompted to orally recount the water cycle. As expected, their answers were short, characterized by bilingual languaging or translanguaging (García & Baetens Beardsmore, 2009) limited to the more observable processes (precipitation and evaporation) expressed through colloquial expressions such as "the water goes up" and "the water goes down," and characterized by the overuse of chronological connectors common in oral interaction such as "and" and "then." Semantically speaking, students' discourse was highly dependent on context (+SG) and expressed in everyday terms (−SD).

Following this and in order to expose students to higher levels of SD, the nominalizations condensation, evaporation, and precipitation were written on the board on top of the diagram drawing lines up and down for evaporation and precipitation respectively. After modeling the use of these important nominalizations—key abstracted nouns that "pack" processes, participants, and circumstances in academic discourses and that "drift" these into "thinginess" and make them prone to "maximum potential for semantic elaboration" (Halliday & Matthiessen, 2006, p. 265)—students were asked to name the Processes and the Participants involved in the cycle for each of the stages, thus denominalizing the concept and spelling out their constituents. For the water cycle stage in which vapor transforms into a denser substance like rain (the highly packed noun "condensation"), Processes such as turn, change, and cool and Participants such as water, drop, liquid, and clouds were mentioned. This process of orally denominalizing (that is, cutting the complex noun or nominalization into more manageable units) highly "packed" nouns such as "condensation" was repeated with other water cycle stages (evaporation and precipitation) orally. This purposeful talk-around text promoted metalinguistic discussions—"grammatics" in Halliday's sense (Halliday, 2002)—as students were both using language to talk about the Processes in question and analyzing the language they were using.

This was accomplished progressively as students grew familiar with the stages of the water cycle, which involved prompting students to dictate the water cycle while I wrote their dictation onto a large sheet of paper following the basic principles of a language experience approach (Nessel & Dixon, 2008). Although still simple, underdeveloped, and highly resembling the oral text, the resulting text was quite different from the highly colloquial oral text produced at the very beginning of the exchange. This first experience reaffirmed the idea that students' familiarity with a concept or topic should not and in fact does not correlate with its disciplinary form. To be recognized as a disciplinary text, it should be structured as a disciplinary text, not only with regards to its content. Indeed, the way in which the message is packaged in language is as important as the message itself!

In the following lesson, we read a short text explaining the water cycle accompanied by the graphic from the previous lesson. After reading the text and checking comprehension, a simple graphic organizer was used for students to complete by identifying the Participants and Processes (Halliday & Matthiessen, 2004) mentioned in the specific water cycle stage (see Figure 5.3 depicting a student's answers for precipitation). This process gave students

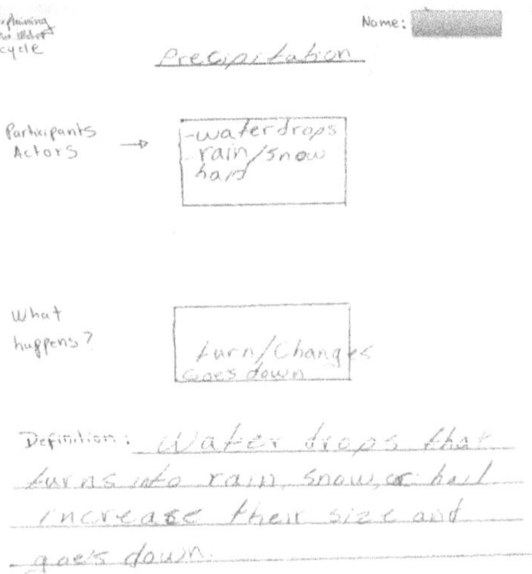

Figure 5.3. Graphic organizer for scaffolding precipitation

further practice with denominalization as a means to unpack written language. Apart from the material Process, "goes down" and the conjunction "and" that reappeared from the simple oral narration, the definition section in Figure 5.3 denotes the emergence of one of the early but important characteristics of scientific discourse in which the nominal group (in this case "water drops that turns into rain, snow, or hail") is extended with an embedded clause (Halliday & Martin, 1996, p. 12). Needless to say that because the development of academic language in the specific discipline and genre are the focus, traditional subject-verb agreement correction and feedback (necessary in the previous embedded clause where a mistake of this kind is evident) become surface issues akin to spelling and punctuation to be addressed on an as needed basis during a later stage of writing.

As the unit progressed, this rich and principled apprenticeship through classroom oral texts was enriched through kineikonic texts ("Seed Growth," 2013), explicit attention to conjunctive and adverbial clauses carrying out time progression (see Figure 5.4), and graphic organizers to scaffold the schematic structure of explanations (see Figure 5.5). Kineikonic texts are characterized by images with animation and multimodal texts which are gaining salience in a multimedia textual environment in which millennial students are immersed (Mills, 2011). These kineikonic texts were manipulated by students illustrating the rock cycle and the seed growth cycle, providing rich comprehensible input in multimodal form that in turn facilitated oral and written output that incorporated some characteristics of academic discourse ("Seed Growth," 2013).

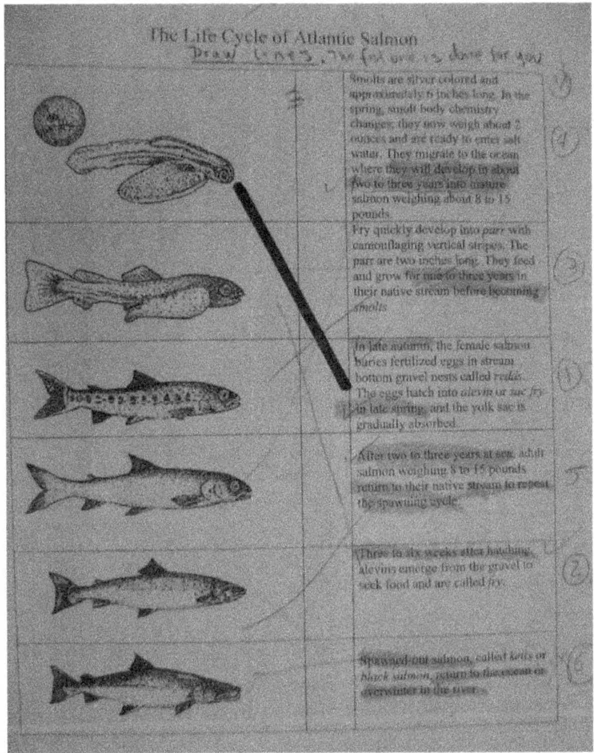

Figure 5.4. The life cycle of the salmon

SEED GROWTH	Text Structure
Seeds are the beginning of a new plant. They need plenty of water and light to grow into a healthy plant.	**Description Stage** What is the function of seeds? What do they need?
When seeds have plenty of water and light, When seeds have plenty of water but not enough light, When seeds have plenty of light but not enough water,	**Explanatory Sequence** What happens to seeds under these different conditions?
	Evaluation or interpretation Why is seed growth important for animals, plants and humans?

Figure 5.5. Seed growth graphic organizer

For consistency, the same graphic organizer already shown with the water cycle example was given and explored, but as students became more comfortable with the scaffolds, the graphic organizers began to change to accommodate the increased complexity of the text. For example, the water cycle graphic organizer changed into one with expanded squares to accommodate all the stages of the rock cycle with only the word "Participants" close to one of the squares and the word "Processes" next to the second square. The accompanying word "Actors" in the first square and the guiding question "What Happens?" present in the first iteration of the graphic organizer were deleted. Students did not seem to have trouble with this minor change, and in fact the graphic organizer for the rock cycle was filled with appropriate words in the "Participants" square such as "magma," "lava chamber," "igneous rocks," and the like. Similarly, the "Processes" square had words like "transform," "replace," "remake," and "evolve," which denoted a higher SD in the context of the abstract process of rock formation (−SG).

To scaffold the schematic structure of Explanations, model texts depicting specific genre stages were first analyzed following exercises that asked students to identify these same stages in other texts. With the help of guided dialogue and highly scaffolded graphic organizers containing full sentences, sentence starters, and text structure stages written on the side (see Figure 5.5), students quickly transitioned into writing full appropriate explanations. As students wrote Explanations on the different focused life cycles, they also were apprenticed into writing more expository texts responding to the unit's idea regarding the interconnection of biological systems as can be seen in the following text written by one of the students.

An ecosystem is a natural unit consisting of all plants, animals, and micro-organisms in an area functioning together with all of the non-living things. Humans and other biological systems are interconnected with ecosystems in complex ways. For example, in the movie we saw "Over the Hedge" the people affected the animal's life by taking their home and their ecosystem. Another example is the extinction of salmon from the Connecticut River around the 1800 hundreds…

In the autumn, the female salmon buries eggs. Three to six weeks later after hatching, they are called fry and quickly develop into Parr with camouflaging vertical stripes. Then after they grow in their stream and then they travel to the ocean. After two to three years, they come back to the river to spawn. The construction of dams, the over fishing, and pollution affected the life cycle of salmon. Now scientists are helping salmon to reproduce in the Connecticut River. In the hatchery, the eggs are incubated and released in to the river.

We should take care of the earth because if we do not plants could die. Plants are important as provide oxygen, clean air, and food. Animals are essential since they give us food and make our environment attractive. Humans, plants and animals are part of one big ecosystem called earth.

Repacking language and removing scaffolds

Providing students with enough practice denominalizing key abstract nouns in lexically dense texts and thus having practice dissecting the elusive grammar of academic discourse as described in the previous section is only one important process toward having these resources become part of the students' repertoire and their own academic identity. Students need practice "repacking" less dense discourse into denser ones, engaging in the purposeful identification, deconstruction, and construction of discourse patterns resembling academic discourse. Two representative discussions illustrate the importance of engaging with students into metalinguistic analysis of this kind. The first was when a comparison between two texts used in the class led to an analysis of the differences between oral and written language. To facilitate this discussion, a reconstruction of some of the utterances that one of the students had used the day before was conducted as a student went to the board to tell the rest of students about the rock cycle as she looked at the animation. During this same class, we were also looking at another text we had read on the rock cycle, which included highly packed nouns such as "igneous crystallization." After comparing the two texts, it became very evident that the oral text was easy for everyone except for one student who was absent that day. As one of the students put it "(name of student) didn't understand because she was not here." In this case, the student was referring to the surprising amount of words in the oral text written on the board that made no sense to the absent student (these were reference words that complemented with the diagram such as *here*, after *that* happens, *it*, *they*, *these* rocks *here*). The discussion centered on the idea that, when we write, we need to be explicit and descriptive of the things we are describing, and we need to use words that carry specific meanings. This need for explicitness, I explained, often results in nouns "packing" a lot of processes and circumstances into a single nominal group such as "igneous crystallization" (+SD) which fully describes the highly abstract and complex processes (–SG) in which 1) magma gets out of its chamber, 2) atoms in melted rock cool, and 3) these atoms then form patterns over long periods of time. We used this example to illustrate how useful it is to be able to pack a lot of meaning into a few words (that is move from −SD +SG to +SD −SG) as to not having to spell out every single process and circumstance involved in this cycle each time we talk about it.

The second illustration of the importance of engaging students into metalinguistic analysis (not as related to the discussion on semantic codes above but as a possible enabler of such a move up and down the semantic continua) happened during an exercise common in the English mainstream class in which students were called to underline all the verbs and circle all the nouns in one of the ecological cycle descriptions we had read. Students were puzzled, and the only insight into approaching this task came from a student who expressed that verbs were actions and nouns were things. This limited (but common) definition did not prove too helpful to get this and other students ahead in accomplishing this simple task. Puzzlement turned into active involvement when, after handing out a text explaining photosynthesis, a text that they had never seen before, students were directed to underline all the Processes and circle all the Participants. By this time, students had already had the opportunity to highlight the Circumstances in a previous text, so they also had to do this. Students picked up and used their highlighters, then their pencils and then their highlighters again. When the highlighting and underlining receded after a few minutes, one of the students raised his hand asking me to come to her. Smiling, she whispered to my ear in perfect Spanglish: "Mister, los verbs son los Processes y los nouns son los Participants, verdad?" (the verbs are the Processes and the nouns are the Participants, right?). Invigorated by this meaningful and powerful recontextualization directly afforded by SFL terminology—ironically often the target of reductionist and ill informed criticisms (see, for example, Martin, 2008)—I assented discretely and beamed back. Albeit by no means complete or complex, a small but significant victory had been won: their academic ontogenesis was under way.

Conclusion

Despite their humanistic appeal and wide use in ESL methodologies, constructivist principles as traditionally understood and applied in the U.S.A. may benefit greatly from an enhanced literacy studies framework of a textually mediated social world and its essential role for understanding and analyzing contemporary changes in language use (Barton, 2001). As evident in this chapter, and under the Strategic Alignment framework, the institutional mandates were radically transformed to serve the needs, rights, and backgrounds of students without losing sight of what was required academically of them. The academic ontogenesis described in this chapter owes much to a Strategic Alignment position that in this classroom essentially utilized the multiple and appropriate affordances of a functional approach to language, including the explicit semantic codes from Legitimation Code Theory. Together, they serve as a "a tool kit for exploring language in use" (Macken-Horarik, 2006), an explicit metalanguage—or "grammatics" as Halliday calls it (Halliday, 2002)—that affords its users to explicitly talk not only about what texts mean, but how authors build what they mean. This position indeed assumes that curriculum exists only in language, in the texts that students are expected to read and write, and in the oral discourse of the classrooms where recontextualization of these texts into "pedagogic discourse" happens (Rose, 2011).

The educational focus of this approach hands teachers and students the language to track closely the meanings embodied in written texts, providing a unique orientation that focuses on what students can do, identifying their strengths and making clear and positive suggestions as to how to make their texts more effective. This approach helps practitioners move away from a knowledge blindness position overtaken by an overreliance on the knowers with a rhetoric of deficiencies to be remedied, a discourse of mistakes, risk or "lack," and to resist serving as simple facilitators or passive spectators surrendered to quasi biological development, waiting for the parts to come "naturally later." It is also important to highlight that this kind of pedagogy hands back teachers their rightful and essential but sometimes disputed place in essential apprenticeship of students into gaining more control of over language, as they are called to design more sophisticated texts to match the increasingly complex knowledge they should handle in the disciplines (Christie & Derewianka, 2008).

Foregrounding disciplinary knowledge building is overdue in U.S. educational reform. It is not surprising that it has taken too long to make its way in if against the background of the futile debates described in this chapter we add the highly dominant linguistic perspectives advanced by Noam Chomsky. Without dwelling on the lack of focus on disciplinary knowledge in his model, the education of ELLs or ELLs themselves was a population that Chomsky's ideal model of language could have never accounted for. Indeed, it is of special importance to ELLs and their teachers that functional grammar compels a pedagogy that is maximally supportive initially and allows for handover when students have appropriated text and language knowledge and know-how (Macken-Horarik et al., 2011). Without the pedagogical principles of Strategic Alignment and genre-based pedagogy, instruction for ELL students at Pleasant Valley would have resembled the inadequacies common to instruction of ELLs. As expressed in Martin and Rose (2008), in Halliday's linguistics, theory emerges out of a dialectic with practice. This chapter has sought to contribute, if only a little, to such an endeavor.

References

Allington, R. L. (2002). *Big brother and the national reading curriculum: How ideology trumped evidence*. Portsmouth, NH: Heinemann.

Artiles, A., Klingner, J., Sullivan, A., & Firerros, E. (2010). Shifting landscapes of professional practices: English learner special education placement in English-only states. In *Forbidden language : English learners and restrictive language policies* (pp. 102–117). New York: Teachers College Press.

Baker, B. (2010). *The pendulum swings: Transforming school reform.* New York: Stylus Publishing.

Barton, D. (2001). Directions for literacy research: Analysing language and social practices in a textually mediated world. *Language and Education, 15*(2 & 3). http://dx.doi.org/10.1080/09500780108666803

Bernstein, B. B. (2000). *Pedagogy, symbolic control, and identity: Theory, research, critique* (Rev. ed.). Lanham, MD: Rowman & Littlefield Publishers.

Christie, F. (2002). *Classroom discourse analysis: A functional perspective.* London: Continuum.

Christie, F. (2004). Authority and its role in the pedagogic relationship of schooling. In L. Young & C. Harrison (Eds.), *Systemic functional linguistics and critical discourse analysis: Studies in social change* (pp. 173–201). London: Continuum.

Christie, F., & Derewianka, B. (2008). *School discourse: Learning to write across the years of schooling.* London: Continuum.

Christie, F., & Maton, K. (2011). *Disciplinarity functional linguistics and sociological perspectives.* London: Continuum.

Crawford, J., & Educational Resources Information Center (U.S.). (1997). Best evidence Research Foundations of the Bilingual Education Act NCBE report (pp. 1 v.). Retrieved from http://www.eric.ed.gov/contentdelivery/servlet/ERICServlet?accno=ED408858

Delpit, L. D. (1995). *Other people's children: Cultural conflict in the classroom.* New York: New Press.

Delpit, L. D. (2012). *"Multiplication is for white people": Raising expectations for other people's children.* New York: New Press.

Derewianka, B. (2000). *Exploring how texts work.* Sydney: Primary English Teaching Association.

Eldesky, C., & Bomer, A. (2005). Heads they win; Tails we lose. In B. Altwerger (Ed.), *Reading for profit: How the bottom line leaves kids behind* (pp. 11–20). Portsmouth, NH: Heinemann.

García, O., & Baetens Beardsmore, H. (2009). *Bilingual education in the 21st century: A global perspective.* Malden, MA: Wiley-Blackwell.

García, O., & Kleifgen, J. A. (2010). *Educating emergent bilinguals: Policies, programs, and practices for English language learners.* New York: Teachers College Press.

Giroux, H. A. (2001). *Theory and resistance in education: Towards a pedagogy for the opposition* (Rev. and expanded ed.). Westport, CT: Bergin & Garvey.

Gutiérrez, K. D., & Jaramillo, N. E. (2006). Looking for educational equity: The consequences of relying on Brown. *Yearbook of the National Society for the Study of Education, 105*, 173–189 doi: 110.1111/j.1744-7984.2006.00081.x.

Halliday, M. A. K. (2002). On grammar and grammatics. In J. Webster (Ed.), *The collected works of M A K Halliday* (pp. 384–417). London: Continuum.

Halliday, M. A. K., & Martin, J. R. (1996). *Writing science: Literacy and discursive power.* London: Falmer Press.

Halliday, M. A. K., & Matthiessen, C. M. I. M. (2004). *An introduction to functional grammar* (3rd ed.). London: Arnold.

Halliday, M. A. K., & Matthiessen, C. M. I. M. (2006). *Construing experience through meaning: A language-based approach to cognition.* London: Continuum.

Hasan, R. (1999). Society, language and the mind: The meta-dialogism of Basil Bernstein's theory. In F. Christie (Ed.), *Open linguistics series* (pp. 10–30). London: Cassell.

Kim, J. (2011). *Relationships among and between ELL status, demographic characteristics, enrollment history, and school persistence* (CRESST Report 810). Los Angeles: University of California, National Center for Research on Evaluation, Standards, and Student Testing (CRESST).

Krashen, S. (2004). False claims about literacy development. *Educational Leadership, 61*(6), 18–21.

Lemke, J. (1990). *Talking science: Language, learning, and values*. Norwood, NJ: Ablex Publishing Corporation.

Lipman, P. (2004). *High stakes education: Inequality, globalization, and urban school reform*. New York: RoutledgeFalmer.

Luke, A. (1996). Genres of power? Literacy education and the production of capital. In R. Hasan & G. Williams (Eds.), *Literacy in society* (pp. 308–338). New York: Adysson Wesley.

Macken-Horarik, M. (2006). Knowledge through "know how": Systemic functional grammatics and the symbolic reading. *English Teaching: Practice and Critique, 5*(1), 102–121.

Macken-Horarik, M., Adoniou, M., de Oliveira, L. C., & Ramirez, J. A. (2011). *Teaching that works*. Paper presented at the TESOL International Conference, New Orleans.

Magnet School Assistance (n.d.). In U.S. Department of Education. Retrieved from http://www2.ed.gov/programs/magnet/index.html

Martin, J. R. (2008). Incongruent and proud. *Discourse & Society, 19*(6), 827–836.

Martin, J. R., & Rose, D. (2008). *Genre relations: Mapping culture*. Oakville, CT: Equinox.

Maton, K. (2011). *Theories and things: The semantics of disciplinarity*. New York: Continuum.

Maton, K. (2013). Making semantic waves: A key to cumulative knowledge-building. *Linguistics and Education, 24*, 8–22.

Mills, K. (2011). "Now I know their secrets": Kineikonic texts in the literacy classroom. *Australian Journal of Language and Literacy, 34*(1), 24–37.

Moje, E., & Speyer, J. (2008). The reality of challenging texts in high school science and social studies: How teachers can mediate comprehension. In K. Hinchman & H. Sheridan-Thomas (Eds.), *Best practices in adolescent literacy instruction* (pp. 185–211). New York: Guilford.

Nessel, D., & Dixon, C. (2008). *Using the language experience approach with English language learners: Strategies for engaging students and developing literacy*. Thousand Oaks, CA: Corwin Press.

Ovando, C. J., Collier, V. P., & Combs, M. C. (2003). *Bilingual and ESL classrooms: Teaching in multicultural contexts* (3rd ed.). Boston, MA: McGraw-Hill.

Ramanathan, V. (2002). *The politics of TESOL education: Writing, knowledge, critical pedagogy*. New York: RoutledgeFalmer.

Ramirez, J. A. (2008). *Co-constructing a nurturing and culturally relevant academic environment for struggling readers: (Dis)locating crisis and risk through strategic alignment (Ed.D)*, Electronic Doctoral Dissertations for the University of Massachusetts-Amherst. Retrieved from http://scholarworks.umass.edu/dissertations/AAI3325279 (Paper AAI3325279.)

Rodby, J. (1992). *Appropriating literacy: Writing and reading in English as a second language*. Portsmouth, NH: Boynton/Cook.

Rose, D. (2011). Beyond literacy: Building an integrated pedagogic genre. *Australian Journal of Language and Literacy, 34*(1), 81–97.

Rose, D., & Martin, J. R. (2012). *Learning to write, reading to learn: Genre, knowledge and pedagogy in the Sydney school*. Bristol, CT: Equinox.

Rothery, J. (1996). Making changes: developing an educational linguistics. In R. Hasan & G. Williams (Eds.), *Literacy in society*. London: Longman.

Schleppegrell, M. (2004). *The language of schooling: A functional linguistics perspective*. Mahwah, NJ: Lawrence Erlbaum Associates.

Seed Growth. (2013). Retrieved May 2013, from http://www2.bgfl.org/bgfl2/custom/resources_ftp/client_ftp/ks2/science/plants_pt2/growth.htm

Shor, I., & Pari, C. (1999). *Critical literacy in action: Writing words, changing worlds*. Portsmouth, NH: Boynton/Cook/Heinemann.

Short, D., & Fitzsimmons, S. (2007). *Double the work: Challenges and solutions to acquiring language and academic literacy for adolescent English language learners*. New York: Carnegie Corporation of New York.

Snow, A., Met, M., & Genesee, F. (1989). A conceptual framework for the integration of language and content in second/foreign language instruction. *TESOL Quarterly, 23*(2), 201–217.

Strong, G., Torgerson, C. J., Torgerson, D., & Hulme, C. (2011). A systematic meta-analytic review of evidence for the effectiveness of the "Fast ForWord" language intervention program. *Journal of Child Psychology and Psychiatry, 52*(3), 224–235.

Thomas, W. P., & Collier, V. P. (1997). *School effectiveness for language minority students* (Vol. 9). National Clearinghouse for English Language Acquisition (NCELA) Resource Collection Series

Weis, L. (1988). *Class, race, and gender in American education*. Albany, NY: State University of New York Press.

6 Critical systemic functional linguistics and the teaching of literary narratives in secondary school English

Ruth Harman and Amber M. Simmons

In recent years, even though genre awareness is seen as a key component in academic literacy development for both first (L1) and second (L2) language learners, very little research has focused on how secondary school teachers develop language curricula based on a dynamic and nuanced view of register and genre (Christie & Macken-Horarik, 2011; Gebhard & Harman, 2011; Hyland, 2004; Tardy, 2006). Christie and Macken-Horarik, for example, discuss how the metalanguage offered to secondary school students in subject English is often arbitrarily applied, thus providing students with few resources to articulate clearly their appreciation of specific text types and configurations of meanings. Because students are expected to respond to literary and other texts in very nuanced and specific ways (e.g., cultural studies), their lack of metalanguage can dramatically impact how they are rated in high-stakes testing and in their transition to university contexts (see Macken-Horarik, 2006; Rothery & Stenglin, 2000).

Fang and Schleppegrell (2008), among a large number of language researchers, see systemic functional linguistics (SFL) as an effective way to generate a dynamic view of language and genre among mainstream and language educators. For SFL scholars, a functional linguistic approach to language and literacy development in school settings allows scholars and teachers to analyze a school's *recontextualization* of multiple discourses, explore the shifts between everyday and academic registers (see Halliday, 1996), and make the hidden assumptions and cultural values in the curriculum more transparent. For example, Schleppegrell and her colleagues in the California History Project (e.g., Achugar, Schleppegrell, & Oteíza, 2007; de Oliveira, 2011, 2012; Schleppegrell, Achugar, & Oteíza, 2004; Schleppegrell & de Oliveira, 2006) worked with history and English teachers in California to identify the language and rhetorical structures in disciplinary texts and to explore how this linguistic knowledge could be used in designing a "language-based content pedagogy" that supported striving readers and language learners in gaining more equitable and explicit access to advanced academic literacy (Fang & Schleppegrell, 2008).

However, little SFL research has focused on how content area teachers engage with students as *critical* text analysts, even if critical meta-awareness has been shown to afford learners with pivotal resources to appropriate and challenge dominant knowledge domains in our increasingly discursive society (e.g., Gebhard, Demers, & Castillo-Rosenthal, 2008; Harman, 2008; Morgan & Ramanthan, 2005; Pennycook, 2001; Simmons, 2012). In this chapter, we show how Amber's critical SFL pedagogy with her upper level secondary school students in subject English supported their use of SFL in analyzing how particular patterns of meaning in literary texts enact a particular evaluative and ideological stance in building characterization and world view (e.g., Lukin, 2008; Macken-Horarik, 2003; Rothery, 1996; Unsworth, 2002). In other words, through critical language-based literary instruction, students were taught to see the "meaning-making capacity of language" (Byrnes, 2006, p.17) and how it is used ideologically (Harman, 2013; Simmons, 2012).

We begin with a description of our theoretical approach and a brief literature review of critical approaches to SFL in fostering critical metalinguistic awareness among K–12 students in subject English. We then describe the critical language approach that Amber developed over time in her Advanced Placement (AP) Language and Composition course and illustrate how the culturally diverse group of students learned to analyze Rowling's (1997) fiction using the SFL interpersonal register metafunction. Amber developed her approach while taking a critical discourse analysis course at the University of Georgia taught by Ruth. In our concluding section, we discuss the importance of using critical SFL approaches in K–12 and in teacher education classrooms.

A critical sociocultural and SFL perspective on teaching literary fiction

As Martin (2000) conceptualizes it, linguistic praxis develops over time through a recursive engagement with theory about language and through practice in the field. Amber's pedagogical approach and our overall conceptual framework in this study are informed by a sociocultural (SCT) and SFL perspective on meaning making that we developed through immersion in theories and reflexive application of these theories in classroom instruction (Halliday & Matthiesen, 2004; Vygotsky, 1978; Wertsch, 1998). SCT emphasizes the role of social interaction and cultural artifacts such as a student's metalanguage as key tools in mediating changes in an individual's cognitive understanding of how and what to communicate in particular sociocultural contexts (Moll, 2001).

Connected to this sociocultural perspective on learning, the functional oriented theory of SFL supports educators and students in seeing text as a recurrent grouping and systematic staging of discourse semantic processes enacted by members of specific cultural discourse communities to achieve social and academic goals. Amber and her students, for example, used SFL analytic resources to explore how patterns of appraisal (e.g., attitude, graduation) helped in construing particular types of characters and ideological world views in literary texts. As Toolan (1988) remarks, through this type of nuanced discourse analysis, readers "rapidly obtain a preliminary picture of who is agentive, who is affected, whether characters are doers or thinkers, whether instruments and forces in the world dominate in the representation" (p. 115).

To support teachers in applying sociocultural and SFL approaches to literacy instruction in subject English, educational linguists in Sydney developed the teaching/learning cycle in the 1990s (Macken-Horarik, 2002; Rothery, 1996). As Martin and Rose (2005) describe it, the first phase in the cycle, a *deconstruction phase*, involves developing learners' understanding of a new subject matter, or "field," and the context of the particular genre the students will read or write (e.g., Science Report, Narrative, Historical Account). Teacher and students generate this knowledge through discussion, analysis of the patterns of linguistic choices and genre moves in sample texts, and experiential activities. In the second stage of *joint construction*, students are encouraged to write about the subject area with the active participation of their teacher. In the final stage of the cycle, students apply their learning of how to build field, tenor, and mode in specific academic genres by writing independent texts. Rothery and Stenglin (1994) highlight how this cyclical teaching can support a more *critical orientation* to reading and writing texts.

To illustrate this approach, in an important SFL-informed action research study undertaken in the Write It Right program in Australia, Rothery (1996) worked with middle school English teachers on literary narratives. In developing the curriculum, they started by working on everyday forms of narrative (e.g., traditional stories with one field and expected types of counter expectancy and complications, a structure that is more congruent with oral storytelling). They slowly moved to a reading and analysis of more complex types of narrative and configurations of meanings (e.g., science fiction where two fields are set in opposition to one another and counter expectant phrases of the genre continually shift the expected trajectory of the story). According to Rothery (1996), the collaborative genre analysis "opens up the possibility of challenging ideologies which so often seem 'natural' in the culture" (p. 119).

Purpose of using a critical SFL approach with AP students

Recent SFL work on academic literacies has explored school discourses from a critical perspective, especially on how particular linguistic resources are used to make particular patterns of meanings in institutional settings (e.g., Christie & Macken-Horarik, 2007; Harman, 2013; Humphrey, Love, & Droga, 2011; Macken-Horarik, Love, & Unsworth, 2011; Unsworth, 2002). Specific to subject English literary fiction, Amber's pedagogical approach was informed by the SFL literary research and praxis of SFL scholars (e.g., Macken-Horarik, 1998, 2003; Martin & Rose, 2003, 2008; Rothery & Stenglin, 1997) who focus on how particular patterns of meaning (e.g., appraisal, transitivity) are deployed in distinct phases of a genre sequence (e.g., Description, Reaction, Problem) to engage the reader in the unfolding of a story (Martin & Rose, 2008, p.82) and to create particular ideological world views (Fowler, 1986).

Specifically, Amber and her students explored how a range of appraisal and identification resources functioned in prosodically coordinated ways in Rowling's *Harry Potter and the Sorcerer's Stone* (1997). Amber chose to focus on analysis of the author's patterned use of these interpersonal and textual resources because she felt students needed more apprenticeship in seeing and articulating how subtle changes in evaluation are used by authors to vilify, ratify, or normalize particular characters or points of view in fiction and expository texts. Specifically, the appraisal system developed by Martin and Rose (2003, 2008) and Martin and White (2005) provided Amber and her students with resources to explore how Attitude, Judgment, and Appreciation of characters and setting were inscribed and invoked in the fantasy genre. Identification analysis also helped them in this regard as it supported their tracking of how Participants were classified and described throughout the text, thus providing key information about how gender, class, and race were being socially constructed in the unfolding of the genre sequences (Jackson, 1990; Martin & Rose, 2003).

Amber's curriculum cycle

In order to support students' development in both the usage of SFL tools as well as critical awareness, Amber designed a curriculum that was informed by Rothery and Stenglin's (1994) teaching and learning pedagogical cycle. Figure 6.1 below shows the four different stages of Amber's curriculum.

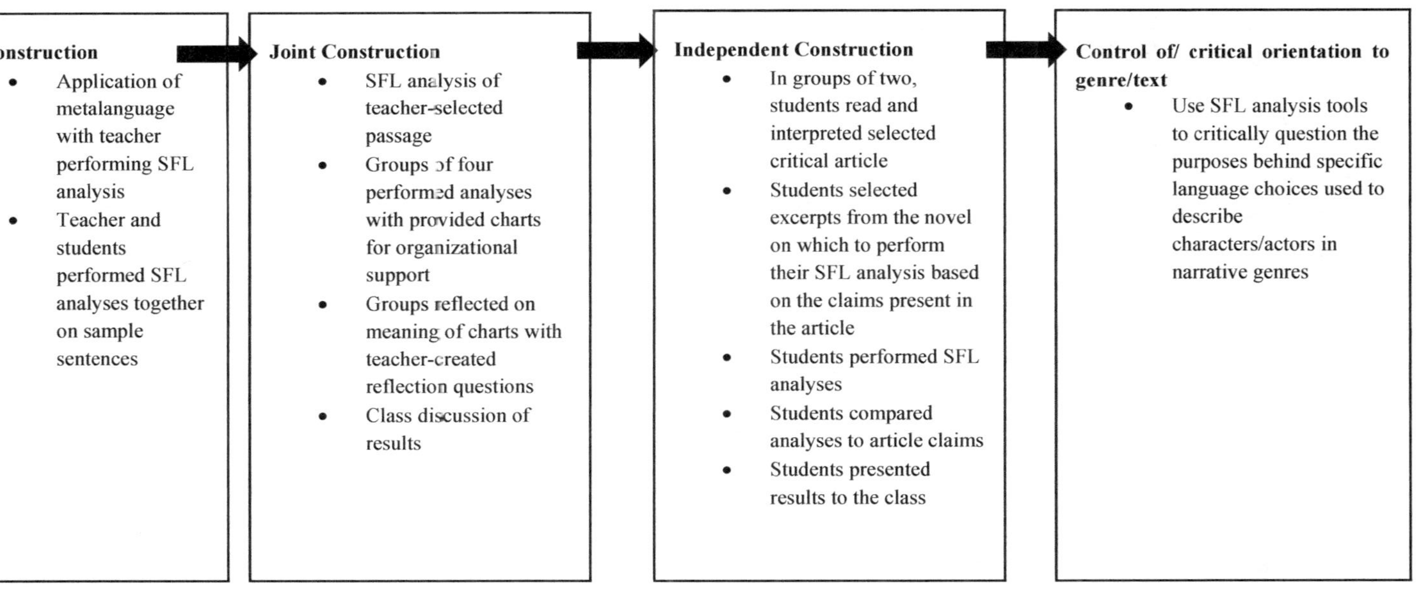

Figure 6.1. Amber's curriculum cycle

Deconstruction: direct instruction and teacher modeling

In the spring of 2012, 60 AP language and composition students in a southeastern suburban school participated in a critical SFL analysis of *Harry Potter and the Sorcerer's Stone* (Rowling, 1997). The diverse group of AP students in two separate classes first read the novel *Harry Potter*, reading a few chapters each night and discussing their interpretation/understanding in small groups of four and then sharing what they perceived to be their most insightful observations with the whole class. After students completed the novel, Amber began the curriculum cycle with the description stage, introducing students to SFL metadiscourse through direct instruction and teacher demonstrations. When demonstrating how to perform appraisal and identification analysis, Amber focused on sections of the novel that introduced new characters, using SFL to show students how language analysis could reveal how the author was making readers feel toward particular characters.

Because of the complex nature of SFL discourse analysis and the limited amount of time Amber had with her students to enhance their literary appreciation (only four months), in the curriculum cycle she decided to show students how inscribed (i.e., explicit) and invoked (i.e., implicit) appraisal functioned together in extended stretches of text to convey a particular Judgment or evaluative stance to or within a character. In other words, instead of coding each appraisal resource in a clause individually, the students were taught to look at the overall appraisal and lexico-grammatical patterns in stretches of discourse (e.g., modality, mental and behavioral Processes, amplified Adjuncts) to see how they functioned in building evaluative stance toward setting and characterization.

For example (see Table 6.1 below), when teaching the students how they would code for appraisal, Amber used Rowling's introductory characterization of Mr. Dursley to illustrate how the invoked appraisal of Affect realized through use of the behavioral Process "humming" and the inscribed Appreciation realized through the amplified Epithet "most boring tie" functioned together across a stretch of discourse to naturalize a particular judgment of Mr. Dursley's personality and self-perception. Through a focus on the prosodic realization of evaluation in the passage, in other words, students were taught to analyze how the inscribed Appreciation and invoked Affect create a picture of a self-satisfied Mr. Dursley who is content with his perceived position as a member of the status quo and his general position in life, however mundane. As Martin and White (2005) highlighted, "attitudinal meanings spread out and color a phrase of discourse as speakers and writers take up a stance oriented to affect, judgment and appreciation" (p. 43).

Table 6.1. Examples used by Amber to familiarize students with interpersonal resources

Analysis type	**Genre sequence/ phase**	**Quote from text**	**Coding of quote**	**Critical analysis/ reflection of coding**
Appraisal coding: Invoked affect **bold** Invoked judgment <u>underlined</u> Inscribed appreciation *italics*	*Description phase in Chapter 1:* Introduction to the Dursley's and the characters of Vernon, Petunia, and Dudley.	"Mr. Dursley hummed as he picked out his most boring tie for work and Mrs. Dursley gossiped away happily as she wrestled a screaming Dudley into his high chair" (Rowling, 1997, p. 2).	"Mr. Dursley **hummed** as he picked out his *most* <u>boring</u> tie for work and Mrs. Dursley <u>gossiped</u> away **happily** as she wrestled a <u>screaming</u> Dudley into his high chair" (Rowling, 1997, p. 2).	This appraisal analysis not only gives information as to the habits and personalities of the Dursley's, but also society's view of what is considered a "normal" family unit. The father goes to work while the mother stays home and takes care of the baby. It also reinforces the stereotypes of the "working stiff," gossipy homemaker, and misbehaved child.
Modality coding: Modal verbs **bold**	*Description phase in chapter 8:* Introduction of Snape's class (Potions) and his abilities/job	"I can teach you how to bottle fame, brew glory, even stopper death—if you aren't as big a bunch of dunderheads as I usually have to teach" (Rowling, 1997, p. 137).	"I **can** teach you how to bottle fame, brew glory, even stopper death—if you aren't as big a bunch of dunderheads as I usually **have** to teach" (Rowling, 1997, p.137).	This modality analysis shows that Professor Snape is in a position of power. He has the power to choose whether or not to share his knowledge with his students. In essence he *can* if he so desires; he doesn't *have* to or necessarily *want* to. This suggests that he is a character who might abuse his power over the students throughout the series. In addition, the analysis shows how he feels about teaching—it is something he *has* to do, not something he *gets/wants/loves* to do. This modality analysis helps establish Snape as an antagonist throughout the novel.

Identification coding: Nouns and pronouns **bold**	*Description phase in* Deathly Hallows*:* Introduction of Kreacher and Harry's history with him	"He would have found Kreacher, with his snoutlike nose and bloodshot eyes, a distinctly unlovable object even if the elf had not betrayed Sirius to Voldemort" (Rowling, 1997, p.191).	"**He** would have found **Kreacher**, with **his** snoutlike nose and bloodshot eyes, a distinctly unlovable **object** even if the **elf** had not betrayed **Sirius** to **Voldemort**" (Rowling, 1997, p.191).	An identification analysis confirms the claim that Harry Potter does not view Kreacher as worthy of respect and courtesy. While Rowling mentioned Kreacher's proper name, which is generally a sign of respect, he is referred to with a pronoun once, as an "elf" once, and once as an "object." The author is constantly reminding the reader of Kreacher's lesser status, that of non-human by using such words to identify him.

In a second phase of deconstruction, Amber invited the students to support her in conducting SFL analyses on similar stretches of discourse that described the same characters from this first passage (see Table 6.1 above): the Dursley's, Snape, and Kreacher.

Joint construction: group practice with teacher support

After a week of participating in deconstruction of particular stretches of discourse, the second phase of the curriculum cycle involved students applying their SFL analysis skills to a teacher-selected passage from the novel. To support students' understanding of how the interpersonal metafunction builds characterization, the passage focused on descriptions and classification of the Hogwarts students. The language in this section was particularly conducive to utilizing SFL tools to determine how Rowling used particular linguistic choices to get readers to side with Harry and his friends and against Draco and his gang (see Table 6.2). This joint construction stage of the coding process proved essential because Amber felt it gave students an organized format in which to practice performing appraisal, identification, and modality analyses in a large group setting with teacher support before attempting it in smaller groups, also providing them with an example to look at as they worked on their project. From an SFL perspective, Amber could see that their analyses (e.g., Table 6.2) sometimes inaccurately coded appraisal resources or failed to

Table 6.2. Sample of students' joint SFL analyses

Student appraisal categories	Code
Affect	**bold**
Judgment	underline
Appreciation	*italics*

"Is it true." he said. "They're saying all down the train that Harry Potter's in this compartment. So it's you, is it." "Yes," said Harry. He was looking at the other boys. Both of them were thickset and looked *extremely* **mean**. Standing on either side of the pale boy, they looked like bodyguards.
"Oh, this is Crabbe and this is Goyle," said the pale boy **carelessly**, noticing where Harry was looking. "And my name's Malfoy, Draco Malfoy." Ron gave a slight cough, which might have been **hiding a snigger**. Draco Malfoy looked at him.
"Think my name's funny, do you. No need to ask who you are. My father told me all the Weasleys have red hair, freckles, and more children than they can afford." He turned back to Harry. "You'll soon find out some wizarding families are much better than others, Potter. You don't want to go making friends with the wrong sort. I can help you there." **He held out his hand to shake** Harry's, but Harry didn't take it.
"I think I can tell who the wrong sort are for myself, thanks," he said *coolly*.
Draco Malfoy didn't go red, but a **pink tinge appeared in his pale cheeks**.
"I'd be careful if I were you, Potter," he said *slowly*. "Unless you're a bit politer you'll go the same way as your parents. They didn't know what was good for them, either. You hang around with riffraff like the Weasleys and that Hagrid, and it'll rub off on you."(Rowling, 1997, pp. 108–109)

identify words or phrases that connected to the prosodic coloring of the stretch of discourse (Martin & White, 2005). For example, in Table 6.2, Amber could see that her students did not identify the inscribed Judgment in the following sentence, "You'll soon find out some wizarding families are **much better** than others, Potter." However, from her critical literacy perspective on learning and teaching, Amber felt it was more important to support her novice SFL analysts in learning how to see the ways in which a palette of colors were being used by Rowling to create subtle shades of characterization instead of insisting on complete adherence to SFL terminology. Indeed, the coding conducted by the students over the course of four months showed increasingly nuanced understanding of how language functioned in the novel (Simmons, 2012).

In a metareflection stage of the joint construction of analysis, Amber also provided the students with several reflection questions that supported students in using their novice SFL understandings to develop a critical orientation to the text. Examples of these questions are the following: What did the appraisal analysis reveal about the feelings of the characters during this scene? Are any Judgments made? If so, how do they reveal the feelings the characters have for others or how does the Judgment shape your feelings toward a specific character? Amber's questions also served to show how the students might think about setting up their own inquiry in the independent construction stage of the curriculum cycle.

In reflecting on these questions and relating them to their analysis in Table 6.2, for example, students discussed how the pattern of Affect words construe the interrelationship between the two groups of boys as confrontational and position Harry clearly on the same side as Ron, setting up the dichotomy for the rest of the Harry Potter series: Slytherin vs. Gryffindor. Students also noted that Rowling intentionally used negative Judgment words to describe Malfoy ("pale") and Crabbe and Goyle ("extremely mean" and "bodyguards") to characterize them as the antagonists in the narrative. While Ron is also described with negative Judgments, students noticed that the purpose and intent were different. When Malfoy calls Ron "riffraff" and the "wrong sort," readers sympathize with Ron because he is being judged by his socio-economic status ("more children than they can afford") and culturally "othered" appearance in the particular sociopolitical setting of the novel ("red hair and freckles"), not his character. In other words, the students began to see how particular chains of lexical relations and patterns of discourse semantics are used to create an evaluative texture that naturalize particular literary readings of the characters (Martin & White, 2005). Supporting students in seeing these appraisal patterns and how they function are especially important in literature where texture is created "by linkings, echoes, and correspondences across sections larger than sentences" (Fowler, 1986, p. 9).

Independent construction: Harry Potter *SFL projects*

After the joint construction stage, students were asked to engage in small-group critical discourse analysis of texts. Students in groups of two were encouraged to analyze the connection of the text to a particular sociocultural context, ideological world view, and set of societal power relations (Fairclough, 1992), relying on one another to build understanding instead of the teacher or the entire class (see Figure 6.1 for project requirements). For the *Harry Potter* project, students were asked to choose a published critical essay based on their interests from a list provided by Amber. Essays covered a broad spectrum, ranging from feminist readings of the novel to queer theory. The purpose of reading the literary reviews was to expose students to various critical claims about the novel and invite them to challenge, not just blindly accept, such claims through their own analysis of language.

After reading their selected article, the students made notes on the author's major claims (see Table 6.3 for complete details of the SFL assignment). Students then returned to the primary text, *Harry Potter*, and found examples that reflected or were relevant to the author's claims. They conducted an appraisal analysis and identification analysis to see if J. K. Rowling's language supported or disproved the author's claims. In other words, the students engaged in what Martin and White (2005) call tactical and resistant readings of the novel and the articles. They both engaged in a reading that was used to get at particular evidence in the novel but were also encouraged to resist the interpretations provided by the writers of the reviews, thus engaging in a complex discourse analysis of the primary and secondary texts. Students then presented their findings to the class using PowerPoint or Prezi to stimulate critical discussion.

Table 6.3. Illustrative examples of student work

Harry Potter Project Requirements
***Harry Potter* SFL Discourse Analysis Project** 1. Read your selected critical article. Make notes on the major claims the author is making about the series and the examples they are using to make those claims. 2. Find examples from the book that are relevant to the author's claims. Perform an SFL discourse analysis using an appraisal analysis, identification analysis, and modality analysis to see if J. K. Rowling's language supports or disproves the author's claims. 3. Present your findings to the class to stimulate discussion. **Requirements for PPT presentation** Your presentation provides: 1. A synopsis of the author's claims. 2. Your original reaction to the author's claims. 3. If your author is working within a particular theory (feminist, queer, critical race theory, etc.), provide an overview of how the author defines the theory. 4. For each claim, choose 1–2 examples from the text on which to perform an SFL discourse analysis. Please use all three types of analysis: appraisal, identification, and modality. You do not have to use all three on each example. Choose the analysis for each example that you think will best support or disprove the author's claim. However, you need to have performed all three by the end of your presentation. 5. Show you work: When you do an appraisal analysis, create a code that shows the different elements: affect, judgment, and appreciation (see examples from your notes). Then create a chart like we did with the examples. When you do an identification analysis, underline all nouns and pronouns used to refer to the individuals in question. Create a chart that lists each name per character and how many times it occurs in your selected passage. When you do a modality analysis, underline the words and identify where the words fall on the polarity scale. 6. Discuss with the class what each analysis reveals. Some examples of what you can talk about include: What does the analysis mean? How does it affect your views or interpretation of the novel? What does it mean for the larger genre of children's fantasy literature? What message is being taught? How can it be changed? You can also address other questions that come up.

Becca and Christy[1] selected and analyzed the claims in the critical essay "Class and Socioeconomic Identity in Harry Potter's England" (Park, 2003) by performing an SFL appraisal analysis. Based on the students' interpretation, the article's first claim was that the Harry Potter series portrayed Britain as the "all powerful" empire, as shown through Hogwarts and the Ministry of Magic being located in Britain and all other wizarding schools being portrayed as inferior to Hogwarts. Furthermore, the hierarchy of the teachers and the headmaster of Hogwarts mirrors the classic government of Great Britain, where the division of houses stems from the social caste system. After reading this article, Becca and Christy stated that they had not noticed the strong ties to a British sociopolitical context and ideological world view; however, after reading the critical article and performing a discourse analysis on selected passages of the novel, they found numerous examples that supported Park's claims.

Becca and Christy: analysis 1

As shown in Table 6.4, Becca and Christy conducted an appraisal analysis on the following passage to show evidence of Park's claim that the British social hierarchy is apparent in the *Harry Potter* series:

> I heard he's sort of a savage—lives in a hut on the school grounds and every now and then he gets drunk, tries to do magic, and ends up setting fire to his bed. (Rowling, 1997, p. 78)

Table 6.4. Student coding and explanation of passage

Analysis type	Coded analysis	Critical analysis of coding
Appraisal analysis coding: Inscribed and invoked Affect: **bold** Inscribed and invoked Judgment: <u>underlined</u> Inscribed and invoked Appreciation: *italics*	I heard he's sort of a <u>savage</u>—<u>lives in a hut on the school grounds</u> and every now and then he gets <u>drunk</u>, tries to do magic, and ends up setting fire to his bed. (Rowling, 1997, p. 78)	The judgments in the passage characterize Hagrid as dirty (living in a hut), stupid and uncivilized (savage), and irresponsible and worthless (drunk). The fact that Hagrid does not live in the castle makes the reader view him as an outsider and low in the class system.

[1] Names of students are pseudonyms

In the presentation of the analysis, Becca and Christy explained that the above excerpt illustrates the validity of Park's postcolonial critique of the novel, given that Hagrid is negatively viewed by the upper class as the stereotypical outsider (ignorant and uncivilized) just like Britain once viewed people of other countries (e.g., India, Ireland). However, the presenters also agreed with Park that Harry's acceptance of Hagrid represents the changing views of today's society, which is more accepting of other cultures, and that Malfoy comes across, in this example, as the symbol of old British judgment.

Becca and Christy: analysis 2

Becca and Christy also performed an identification analysis to investigate Park's claim that outsiders to Great Britain are viewed as threats whereas Harry symbolizes the strength and importance of Britain. Table 6.5 illustrates how Becca and Christy tracked the way Voldemort (the outsider and antagonist) is classified and described in comparison with Harry (the symbol of Britain and protagonist).

Table 6.5. Becca and Christy's identification analysis for Voldemort and Harry

Names for Voldemort in chapter 1	Times used	Names for Harry in chapter 5	Times used
Voldemort	6	Harry	14
You-know-who	4	He	3
Him	3	Harry Potter	1
His	2	Mr. Potter	4
He	8	Potter	2

Based on their identification analysis, Becca and Christy concluded that the majority of the time, Voldemort is referred to pronominally while Harry is called by his proper name and in some cases shown respect with the prefix "Mr." Becca and Christy believed that this identification analysis supported Park's observation that the British have grown up believing that other countries are threats, similar to Voldemort's threat to Harry and Hogwarts.

Conclusion

Our discussion of the learning and teaching processes of this critical SFL project illustrates how students began to learn how to analyze the meaning-making resources of language within the Narrative genre with the use of SFL tools over a relatively short period of time. In addition, several students provided Amber with unsolicited feedback on how this pedagogical innovation had larger implications regarding students' desire and ability to apply their incipient SFL knowledge to other Narrative texts outside of the classroom. One student who graduated sent Amber an email that stated, "you taught me how to dissect passages on a whole new level. I've even impressed some of my professors by looking at things with SFL, it's practically ingrained in my conscience!" (Eve, email communication, September 6, 2012). Other student communication with Amber also highlights that student use of SFL analysis tools has not been constrained to the high school classroom but that they have continued to apply critical discourse analysis to their lives, both academic and personal (Simmons, 2012).

Although our reflections on this single case study cannot be used to make generalizations regarding the implications for first or second language literary instruction, certain tentative implications can be drawn. First, Amber's instructional focus on critical literacy and SFL served as a mediating tool for students in noticing and learning about how language is a semiotic process shaped by particular ideological and cultural world views (Wertsch, 1998). Her permeable curricular approach also encouraged students to see discourse analysis as a co-constructed dialogic activity. This finding would tend to support a more systematic use of SFL when providing critical literacy instruction in K-12. Unfortunately, as Christie and Macken-Horarik (2011) and Gebhard and Harman (2011) note, traditional New Literacy Studies and multi-literacies approaches to teaching subject English often do not include critical linguistic analysis of text and context.

Secondly, Unsworth (2000) stresses the need for more SFL research on subject-specific literacies and on critical pedagogies developed from this SFL research. According to Unsworth, researchers need to explicitly analyze the genres and registers in a variety of disciplinary discourses (e.g., Scientific Reports, Literary Narratives, Historical Accounts) and explore how this knowledge can be adapted for use by practitioners. Related to this need for recursive research on the theory and praxis of SFL, we hope that this study's inquiry into the SFL patterns of meaning in literature will foster more research on how to connect language and literature teaching. For example, little research in literary criticism has focused on the connections of specific patterns of meaning to the development of character, point of view, and texture in literary narratives (Culler, 1975).

Thirdly, in the University of Georgia Language and Literacy Department, Amber took courses in critical pedagogy, discourse analysis, and sociocultural theories of learning and teaching. She used this knowledge in designing her multilayered approach to teaching literature. What is remarkable about Amber and her students is how systematically and thoroughly they engaged in collaborative critical discourse analysis and how Amber integrated this linguistic approach with critical literacy. Indeed, our chapter only focuses on one of three literary genres that Amber used in supporting her students' critical SFL learning. We recommend that graduate and teacher education programs support teachers and researchers in developing a similar understanding of critical literacy that involves analyzing the language and content demands of their academic disciplines and how to incorporate the needs and interests of their students in critically meaningful ways (Gebhard, Harman, & Seger, 2007; Harman, 2013; Simmons, 2012; Unsworth, 2000).

References

Achugar, M., Schleppegrell, M., & Oteíza, T. (2007). Engaging teachers in language analysis: A functional linguistics approach to reflective literacy. *English Teaching: Practice and Critique, 6*(2), 8–24.

Byrnes, H. (2006). *Advanced language learning: The contribution of Halliday and Vygotsky*. London: Continuum.

Christie, F., & Macken-Horarik, M. (2007). Building verticality in subject English. In F. Christie & J. R. Martin (Eds.), *Language, knowledge and pedagogy* (pp. 156–183). London: Continuum.

Christie, F., & Macken-Horarik, M. (2011), Disciplinarity and the case of school subject English. In F. Christie & K. Maton (Eds.), *Disciplinarity: Functional linguistic and sociological perspectives* (pp. 175–196). London: Continuum.

Culler, J. (1975). *Structuralist poetics: Structuralism, linguistics, and the study of literature*. London: Routledge. http://dx.doi.org/10.4324/9780203449769

de Oliveira, L. C. (2011). *Knowing and writing school history: The language of students' expository writing and teachers' expectations*. Charlotte, NC: Information Age Publishing.

de Oliveira, L. C. (2012). What history teachers need to know about academic language to teach English language learners. *The Social Studies Review, 51*(1), 76–79.

Fang, Z., & Schleppegrell, M. J. (2008). *Reading in secondary content areas: A language-based pedagogy*. Ann Arbor, MI: University of Michigan Press.

Fairclough, N. (1992). *Discourse and social change*. Malden, MA: Polity Press.

Fowler, R. (1986). *Linguistic criticism*. Oxford: Oxford University Press.

Gebhard, M., Demers, J., & Castillo-Rosenthal, Z. (2008). Teachers as critical text analysts: L2 literacies and teachers' work in the context of high-stakes school reform. *Journal of Second Language Writing, 17*, 274–291. http://dx.doi.org/10.1016/j.jslw.2008.05.001

Gebhard, M., & Harman, R. (2011). Reconsidering genre theory in K–12 schools: A response to school reform in the United States. Special Edition of *Journal of Second Language Writing, 20*(1), 45–55. http://dx.doi.org/10.1016/j.jslw.2010.12.007

Gebhard, M., Harman, R., & Seger, W. (2007). Unpacking academic literacy for ELLs in the context of high-stakes school reform: The potential of systemic functional linguistics. *Language Arts, 85*(5), 419–430.

Halliday, M. A. K. (1996). Literacy and linguistics: A functional perspective. In R. Hasan & G. Williams (Eds.), *Literacy in society* (pp. 339–376). London: Longman.

Halliday, M. A. K., & Matthiesen, C. M. I. M. (2004). *An introduction to functional grammar*. London: Arnold.

Harman, R. (2008). *Systemic functional linguistics and the teaching of literature in urban schools.* Online: Mick O' Donnell (Ed.), International Systemic Functional Linguistics Association. www.isfla.org/Systemics/Print/index.html

Harman, R. (2013) Literary intertextuality in genre-based pedagogies: Building lexical cohesion in fifth-grade L2 writing. *Journal of Second Language Writing, 22*(2), 125–140. http://dx.doi.org/10.1016/j.jslw.2013.03.006

Hyland, K. (2004). *Genre and second language writing.* Ann Arbor, MI: University of Michigan Press.

Humphrey, S., Love, K., & Droga, L. (2011). *Working grammar: An introduction for English teachers*. Melbourne: Pearson Australia.

Jackson, H. (1990). *Grammar and meaning: A semantic approach to English grammar*. London: Longman.

Lukin, A. (2008). Reading literary texts: Beyond personal responses. In Z. Fang & M. J. Schleppegrell (Eds.), *Reading in secondary content areas: A language-based pedagogy* (pp. 84–103). Ann Arbor, MI: University of Michigan Press.

Macken-Horarik, M. (1998). Exploring the requirements of critical school literacy: A view from two classrooms. In F. Christie & R. Misson (Eds.), *Literacy and schooling* (pp. 74–103). London: Routledge.

Macken-Horarik, M. (2002). Something to shoot for: A systemic functional approach to teaching genre in secondary school science. In A. M. Johns (Ed.), *Genres in the classroom: Applying theory and research to practice* (pp. 17–42). Mahwah, NJ: Erlbaum.

Macken-Horarik, M. (2003). Appraisal and the special instructiveness of narrative. *Text, 23*(2), 285–312. http://dx.doi.org/10.1515/text.2003.012

Macken-Horarik, M. (2006). Knowledge through "know how": Systemic functional grammatics and the symbolic reading. *English Teaching: Practice and Critique, 5*(1), 102–121.

Macken-Horarik, M., Love, K., & Unsworth, L. (2011). A grammatics "good enough" for school English in the 21st century: Four challenges in realising the potential. *Australian Journal of Language and Literacy, 34*(1), 9–23.

Martin, J. R. (2000). Design and practice: Enacting functional linguistics. *Annual Review of Applied Linguistics, 20*, 116–126. http://dx.doi.org/10.1017/S026719050020007X

Martin, J. R., & Rose, D. (2003). *Working with discourse: Meaning beyond the clause*. London: Continuum.

Martin, J. R. & Rose, D. (2005). Designing literacy pedagogy: Scaffolding asymmetries. In R. Hasan, C. M. I. M. Matthiesen, & J. Webster (Eds.), *Continuing discourse on language* (pp. 251–280). London: Equinox.

Martin, J. R., & Rose, D. (2008). *Genre relations: Mapping culture*. Oakville, CT: Equinox.

Martin, J. R., & White, P. R. R. (2005). *The language of evaluation, appraisal in English*. London: Palgrave Macmillan.

Moll, L. C. (2001). The diversity of schooling: A cultural-historical approach. In M. de la Luz Reyes & J. J.Halcon (2001). *The best for our children: Critical perspectives on literacy for Latino students.* Language and literacy series (pp. 13–18). New York: Teachers College Press.

Morgan, B., & Ramanthan, V. (2005). Critical literacies and language education: Global and local perspectives. *Annual Review of Applied Linguistics, 25*, 151–169. http://dx.doi.org/10.1017/S0267190505000085

Park, J. (2003). Class and socioeconomic identity in Harry Potter's England. In G.L. Anatol (Ed.), *Reading Harry Potter: Critical essays* (pp. 179–189). Westport, CT: Greenwood.

Pennycook, A. (2001). *Critical applied linguistics: A critical introduction.* Mahwah, NJ: Lawrence Erlbaum Associates.

Rothery, J. (1996). Making changes: Developing an educational linguistics. In R. Hasan & G. Williams (Eds.), *Literacy in society* (pp. 86–123). London: Longman.

Rothery, J., & Stenglin, M. (1994). *Spine-chilling stories: A unit of work for Junior Secondary English.* Sydney: Metropolitan East Disadvantaged Schools Program.

Rothery, J., & Stenglin, M. (1997). Entertaining and instructing: Exploring experience through story. In F. Christie & J. R. Martin (Eds.), *Genre and institutions: Social processes in the workplace and school* (pp. 231–263). London: Cassell.

Rothery J., & Stenglin, M. (2000). Interpreting literature: The role of appraisal. In L. Unsworth (Ed.), *Researching language in schools and communities: Functional linguistic perspectives* (pp. 222–224). London: Cassell.

Rowling, J. K. (1997). *Harry Potter and the sorcerer's stone*. London: Bloombury.

Schleppegrell, M. J., Achugar, M., & Oteíza, T. (2004). The grammar of history: Enhancing content-based instruction through a functional focus on language. *TESOL Quarterly, 38*(1), 67–93. http://dx.doi.org/10.2307/3588259

Schleppegrell, M. J., & de Oliveira, L. C. (2006). An integrated language and content approach for history teachers. *Journal of English for Academic Purposes, 5*(4), 254–268. http://dx.doi.org/10.1016/j.jeap.2006.08.003

Simmons, A. M. (2012). *Word in the hand: Supporting critical literacy through a discourse analysis of fantasy, canonical, and non-fiction texts.* Unpublished dissertation, University of Georgia.

Tardy, C. M. (2006). Researching first and second language genre learning: A comparative review and a look ahead. *Journal of Second Language Writing, 15*, 79–101. http://dx.doi.org/10.1016/j.jslw.2006.04.003

Toolan, M. (1988). *Narrative: A critical linguistic introduction.* London: Routledge.

Unsworth, L. (2000). *Researching language in schools and communities*. Cassell: London.

Unsworth, L. (2002). Reading grammatically: Exploring the 'constructedness' of literary texts. *L1 Educational Studies of Language and Literature, 2*, 121–140. http://dx.doi.org/10.1023/A:1020847215689

Wertsch, J. V. (1998). *Mind as action.* Oxford: Oxford University Press.

Vygotsky, L. S. (1978). *Mind in society: The development of higher psychological processes*. Cambridge, MA: Harvard University Press.

7 A genre-based approach to teaching the Book Review

Benjamin Boche

The literacy curriculum often experiences a push and pull when it comes to understanding the role of language. One group wants to eradicate the study of language and instead focus on what is more meaningful for the student. Another group recognizes that the study of academic language can only be found in schools and therefore should hold an important place (Cope & Kalantzis, 1993). Regardless, raising genre awareness will not only benefit historically marginalized groups (p. 8), but it will also enable students to negotiate texts they typically encounter in an academic setting. Oftentimes students do not engage in thoughtful reflection on what they are writing in school.

> Unfortunately for our novice students, the texts they produce in their academic classrooms are not as much purposeful as responsive: their instructors assign the tasks and the students respond to them. The students' purposes, in the main, are to please their instructors and/or pass the examinations (Johns, 2008, p. 239).

Therefore, to enable students to not merely reproduce texts but to fully understand their purposes, contexts, and structures, the goal should be to help students understand what literacy curriculum components they will be facing in the future. This is usually most evident in the increasingly complex English classroom.

One of the increasing demands in the English curriculum (Martin & Rose, 2008) is the evaluation of texts. Rothery and Stenglin (1997) described four general types: personal response, review, interpretation, and critical response. Most response types originate as personal response, but as students enter into late childhood and early adolescence, personal responses become less valuable (Martin & Rose, 2008), and the Book Review serves as "a better model for developing students' evaluative capacities" (Christie & Derewianka, 2010, p. 65). Specifically, writing reviews can "prepare the apprentice writer for what is organizationally the more ambitious task in later years, of abstracting away from the text(s) discussed and offering generalizations and/or abstractions about them" (p. 62). Therefore, a close analysis of the genre of the Book Review is needed to help both teachers and students successfully teach and learn to write them, respectively.

This chapter will examine the Book Review genre using an example from a popular writing curriculum, *Write Source*. First, the information *Write Source* provides for teachers in teaching and writing the Book Review will be examined. Teachers familiar with textbooks will no doubt find the characteristics mentioned as nothing new in regards to helping students write, but all of this information provides little insight into the actual genre of a Book Review. Instead, using the lens of systemic functional linguistics to teach the Book Review provides clearer objectives and linguistic awareness for both teachers and students. This awareness will be highlighted in the analysis, teaching/learning cycle section, and the conclusion in this chapter.

Write Source

The Book Review is usually a separate writing assignment in most writing textbooks, and the Book Review discussed in this chapter from *Write Source* (Sebranek, Kemper, & Meyer, 2008) is no exception. *Write Source* defines a Book Review as "a brief essay in which you retell important events in the story, and relate an insight" (p. 289). The objectives for the Book Review *Write Source* outlines are as follows:

- Understand what a Book Review is.
- Understand the form and content of a Book Review.
- Plan, draft, revise, edit, and publish a Book Review.

In order to accomplish these objectives, *Write Source* provides an explanation of a Book Review using the writing traits, a sample text, and a step-by-step process of how to write the different parts of a Book Review.

The writing traits consist of ideas, organization, voice, word choice, sentence fluency, and conventions. For a Book Review, the idea trait includes the focus statement that highlights what the writer's insight is and the importance of supporting it with carefully selected details. The organization of a Book Review usually consists of a chronological order. The voice trait as described in *Write Source* wants writers to use a more formal voice that fits the assignment and the audience, which in this instance are fellow classmates. Word choice means writers pay special attention to the use of active versus passive verbs. There should be concise sentences in regards to sentence fluency, as well as varying sentence beginnings. Finally, for conventions,

Write Source advocates writers should pay special attention to correcting all errors of spelling, punctuation, and grammar.

Write Source uses an example review written by a student focusing on the book *Bud, Not Buddy* (p. 289). While reading, the textbook guides teachers to point out specific features of the Book Review to readers. These include the focus statement at the end of the first paragraph, which reveals the writer's insight. The textbook loosely defines a writer's insight as "gaining an understanding of an important message or idea from the book" (p. 287). This insight is also repeated in the conclusion using different wording yet repeating the most important information. The textbook also points out that the middle paragraphs of a Book Review are summarized in chronological order of the events in the book.

When discussing the writing process, *Write Source* focuses on the prewriting and writing stages. The prewriting stage instructs readers to select a book and create a timeline of events. The textbook then gives readers tips and exercises on how to create a clear focus statement or writer's insight. Finally, the prewriting stage wants writer's to create topic sentences for each of the middle paragraphs. The writing stage encourages writers to use the time line, focus statement, and topic sentences as a guide to writing the actual Book Review. Transitions are also mentioned in order to tie all the writing together.

In addition to the writing process, the beginning, transition words, varying beginnings of sentences, and ending of the Book Review are all given special consideration. *Write Source* explains that the beginning is a general introduction to the story and ends with a focus statement about the book. Transition words are used to indicate time, and the textbook shows writers the different types of words to use in order to provide some variety and yet still accomplish shifts in time. By both explaining and giving examples, *Write Source* wants writers to not be repetitive in the beginnings of sentences in order to add a little variety in the actual writing. The ending of the Book Review restates the writer's insight and the type of message the author wants to leave with the readers. The textbook also indicates that the ending should include how the change in the main character helped develop a writer's insight.

Analysis

The language system is broken down into three metafunctions: the textual metafunction, the ideational metafunction, and the interpersonal metafunction. The textual metafunction involves the language used for the formation of texts. Christie & Derewianka (2010) highlight the importance of the textual function of language in that it "is perhaps the most critical for learners to master as they move from the dynamic and spontaneous oral mode into the more reflective, crafted written texts of schooling" (p. 19). The ideational metafunction looks at language related to experiences and activities and the different Participants in those activities (Christie & Derewianka, 2010). These are represented by various types of Processes involved in the activities. Both the textual metafunction and ideational metafunction will be examined more closely in reference to the Book Review of *Bud, Not Buddy* from *Write Source* presented below. The numbers added in front of each clause are used to indicate the clauses referred to in the analysis.

Bud, Not Buddy

by Jiang Li, student writer

(1) *Bud, Not Buddy* by Christopher Paul Curtis is a story about a young boy finding people who care about him. (2) Like all of us, Bud knows that having people who care for you is a lucky thing. (3) The "family" that Bud finds has some of the same qualities that a lot of families have today. (4) This story shows that some members of a family may not be related, (5) but they still care for each other.

(6) When the story starts, 10-year-old Bud lives with his mother in Flint, Michigan. (7) It is 1936, (8) and the Great Depression is making life hard for most people. (9) Times are very difficult, (10) but they become more difficult for Bud after his mother dies. (11) She never tells him who his father is. (12) Bud thinks a man named Herman E. Calloway may be his father because of five posters his mother has kept through the years. (13) The posters advertise a band named Herman E. Calloway and the Dusky Devastators of the Depression. (14) Bud sets out to find Herman E. Calloway.

(15) Many things happen to Bud as he searches. (16) All of the situations that he comes across show readers what the Great Depression was like. (17) For example, Bud spends time with other homeless people. (18) He tries to leap into a boxcar of a moving train to get to another city. (19) He also waits in food lines and eats at missions. (20) We see how strangers help each other and become like the extended families we have today.

(21) When Bud finally reaches Grand Rapids, he finds Calloway and tells him his story. (22) Calloway says he is not Bud's father. (23) However, he gives Bud jobs in exchange for room and board. (24) Bud doesn't unpack the few things he owns: an old blanket, five smooth rocks with letters and dots written on them, the five posters, and a picture of his mother. (25) Because Calloway is a grumpy, rather mean person, Bud thinks about moving on, (26) but the band members are good to Bud. (27) For one thing, they buy him an old saxophone. (28) This is one of the ways they show Bud they care. (29) The band members know each other's weaknesses and skills. (30) They are a family in many ways, (31) and Bud likes being part of their lives.

(32) The five smooth rocks, not the posters, turn out to be the key to Bud's identity. (33) When Bud discovers that Calloway has a collection of smooth stones in the glove compartment of his car, he tells Calloway, "I've got some of these, sir." (34) Calloway turns out to be his mother's father, not Bud's father, (35) but this makes Calloway his grandfather.

> (36) One of the best parts of the story is when Bud gets his old blanket out and remakes his bed. (37) Now he knows this is the bed his mom slept in as a child. (38) Readers know now that he isn't going to leave. (39) Even though Bud never finds his father, he has found a "family" in the band members and a grouchy grandfather. (40) Not all members of his family are related by blood, (41) but they care for him as any family would (Sebranek, Kemper, & Meyer, 2008, pp. 289–290).

Textual metafunction

The importance of organization in the textual metafunction is crucial in order to relay information to the reader in a cohesive and coherent manner. The Book Review genre has three elements of textual organization:

- *Context:* Provides essential context information, the type of work, and sometimes the setting.
- *Text Description:* Introduces characters and details of the plot.
- *Text Judgment:* Offers the writer's evaluation of the text (Rothery, 1994 as cited in Christie & Derewianka, 2010).

Other important elements in the textual metafunction are clausal Themes (the first part of the clause) and Rhemes (everything after the Theme), their patterns, and the cohesive elements that make up the Book Review genre.

Appendix A shows the Book Review of *Bud, Not Buddy* separated into the three elements mentioned above, as well as showing the Themes and Rhemes of each sentence. Both the Context and the Text Judgment elements of the Book Review are simple paragraphs, while the Text Description element is extended over several paragraphs. Within the Text Description, paragraphs are organized according to chronological time, but do not use explicit words (first, second, last). Instead, time is indicated with different words like *many things happen* (clause 15). Most shifts in chronological time are represented by the word *when* (clauses 6, 21, 33). The word *when* serves its purpose in leading both readers and writers through the major plot elements of the story, but they lack the variety that the textbook wanted the students to use when writing.

For the most part, the text utilizes relatively simple, unmarked Themes. These simple Themes include the subject of the sentence and generally focus on the major characters in the story (i.e., Bud, Calloway, band members). Occasionally the Themes may represent situations that Bud finds himself in or important physical objects like the posters and stones.

Some of the Themes, though, refer to ideas outside of the actual book. For example, the Theme of the Great Depression (clause 8) is a major plot element of *Bud, Not Buddy*, and the writer of the review expects readers to have some knowledge related to this event in history. While the review does provide some clues to this historical event (is making life hard for most people, clause 8), readers unfamiliar with this information may not fully grasp the impact it has on the story plot.

In addition, several Themes refer to information either written earlier or later in the actual review. The Theme *Many things* (clause 15) indicates that readers will have to locate information to make sense of what these "many things" are. The same could be said for the Theme of *The five smooth rocks, not the posters* (clause 32), as it refers to information presented in the previous paragraph that readers and writers will have to remember in order to understand how the plot information fits together. This is also true when the author uses the Theme of *this* (clause 28, 35) to refer to longer pieces of information. Both readers and writers will need to unpack what has been distilled into the word "this" in order to better understand the review.

Marked Themes are present and "foreground a particular angle other than the subject of the clause" (Christie & Derewianka, 2010, p. 21). Marked Themes include larger time clauses such as "When Bud finally reaches Grand Rapids…" The marked Themes in the Book Review *Bud, Not Buddy* highlight shifts in chronological time (i.e., *When the story starts*, clause 6), emphasize character traits (i.e., *Because Calloway is a grumpy, rather mean person,* clause 25), and provide further information about the text (i.e., *For one thing,* clause 27). The importance of examining Themes in a text is to track thematic progression and when the topic is maintained or shifted away by means of marked Themes.

Appendix B shows the different types of cohesive devices employed in the Book Review. Because the writer is trying to convey meaning to a reader, he/she "must try to anticipate what the reader—distanced in time and space—might want to know" (Christie & Derewianka, 2010, p. 22). Appendix B might serve as a good visual representation of the many elements of the textual metafunction mentioned earlier. This Book Review uses a wide range of cohesive devices:

- The personal pronoun *he* refers back to the main characters of *Bud* or *Calloway*.
- The personal pronoun *it* refers back to the *story*.
- The personal pronoun *they* refers back to *family*, *band members*, and *Times*.
- The demonstrative *this* refers back to a sequence of clauses (*they buy him an old saxophone*; *Calloway turns out to be his mother's father*).

While *Bud, Not Buddy* mainly uses simple cohesive devices, the demonstrative *this* referring back to a larger sequence of clauses can cause problems for adolescents. Ultimately the goal is for adolescents to recognize and construct cohesive links between concrete and abstract elements of text.

Ideational metafunction

Each element of Textual Organization (the Context, Text Description, and Text Judgment) uses different Processes as represented in the ideational function to achieve different purposes. The following is a brief description of how the different types of Processes are used in the different organization parts of this Book Review.

As mentioned earlier, the Context provides important information, the genre and sometimes the setting. The author uses relational Processes, *Bud, Not Buddy by Christopher Paul Curtis* ***is*** *a story about a young boy* (clause 1), *The 'family' that Bud finds* ***has*** *some of the same qualities* (clause 3), and *This story* ***shows*** *that some of the members of a family may not be related* (clause 4), to describe and talk about what the book is about. The author uses mental Processes to show how the main characters generally feel and think in the story: *Like all of us, Bud* ***knows*** *that having people who care for you is a lucky thing* (clause 2) and *they still* ***care*** *for each other* (clause 5). The relational and mental Processes are the types of Processes you might expect when establishing a background of a book, as they introduce characters and provide identifying information for readers.

The next stage, the Text Description, introduces key characters, the setting and elements of the plot. While describing the setting, the author mainly uses relational Processes—*It* ***is*** *1936* (clause 7), *the Great Depression* ***is*** *making life hard* (clause 8), *Times* ***are*** *very difficult* (clause 9)—while the subjects are Participants that are being described in the relation. These are similar to the Context stage when the writer was trying to establish the background of the book. When the characters are the subjects, the Processes are either mental (*thinks*, *know*, *likes*) or else they are material and have most of the action (*sets out*, *finds*, *waits*, *gives*, and *unpack*). Characters in the book also speak, so the author also sometimes uses verbal Processes when discussing the characters—*tells* and *says*. The Processes of action, thinking, and saying are usually associated with people, and it makes sense to include these when discussing the characters in the book.

The Text Description stage also discusses the plot, and in this particular book review, the plot is described chronologically. All the information surrounding the plot is realized in time clauses and in Circumstances of time: When the story starts (clause 6), When Bud finally reaches Grand Rapids (clause 21), and When Bud discovers that Calloway has a collection of smooth stones in the glove compartment of his car (clause 33). These chronological indicators of the plot advancing are followed up with material Processes, lives, finds, and a verbal Process, tells. Other plot elements use mainly relational Processes: show, happen, makes.

The final stage in a Book Review is the Text Judgment, where the writer offers an evaluation of the text they are reviewing. When actually describing the story, relational Processes are used: *One of the best parts of the story* ***is*** *when Bud gets his old blanket out and remakes his bed* (clause 36). Because the rest of the Text Judgment stage focuses on the characters in the book, most of the Processes are mental or material as indicative of character thoughts or actions in the book.

Other important Processes to note are when the writer tries to relate back to the people reading the text. Anytime readers are used as Themes, the Processes are always mental: *We* ***see*** *how strangers help each other and become like the extended families we have today* (clause 20) and *Readers* ***know*** *now that he isn't going to leave* (clause 38). Mental Processes are used because readers must comprehend and learn from the text in order to gain these insights. For the most part, the different types of Processes match up with what we would expect. Characters do and think, the readers think about the story, and anytime the book is being talked about, most of the Processes are relational in nature.

Teaching/learning cycle for the Book Review

The teaching/learning cycle highlights the importance of establishing a system of both reading and writing that involves the teacher, students, and the actual text (Rose & Martin, 2012). Based on Rothery and Stenglin's (1997) secondary school English materials, the teaching/learning cycle and subsequent detailed reading involves different phases of activity that move both the students and teachers through different cycles of scaffolding that help deconstruct and reconstruct different genres. While *Write Source* may provide different sections for students to work on as part of the Book Review, what is missing is the initial detailed reading to help students understand the genre and the linguistic features of the text.

Detailed reading helps learners recognize a text's genre and field in order to gain "enough experience to interpret the field as it unfolds through the text" (Martin & Rose, 2005, p. 258). Therefore, detailed reading consists of three cycles: Prepare, Identify, and Elaborate. The Preparation phase would consist of reading through the book review as a class and looking at its genre structure, how it unfolds throughout, and providing a quick summary of how the review is organized. *Write Source* does provide a useful model for the class to look at, but teachers must then move students into the next phase, Identify, without any guidance. In the Identification stage, meanings at the sentence level are examined, and teachers can "provide adequate support to recognize wordings from the perspective of meaning" (p. 258). With this new knowledge, students are able to elaborate upon technical aspects of the Book Review and relate any relevant information or new concepts learned throughout the process. By including a detailed reading while looking at a specific genre, students will have the necessary skills to be successful in the teaching/learning cycle.

The teaching/learning cycle consists of three phases. Deconstruction "foregrounds modeling, establishing one genre or another as a goal for the cycle as a whole" (p. 252). Joint Construction seeks input from the students in order to create a new example of the genre. Students are then responsible for creating their own new text of the same genre in the last stage, Individual Reconstruction. Even though *Write Source* first showcases an example text for the teacher and students to look at in the Deconstruction cycle, there is no discussion of the specific field and context of the Book Review. Therefore, students may struggle with identifying features such as textual organization, different Processes used, and cohesion.

What is completely lacking in *Write Source* is the opportunity for Joint Construction and creating a shared experience with both the students and teachers. Shared experience is:

> engendered by establishing clear generic goals, building field and setting context; interaction is built into teaching and learning, in the design of various field building experiences and the Joint Construction phase in particular; and the teacher is regularly placed in an authoritative position as far as guidance is concerned—whether modeling the genre, recontextualising spoken student discourse as writing when scribing or scaffolding field building activities (Martin & Rose, 2005, pp. 252–253).

Without the Joint Construction stage, students may enter into the Individual Construction stage of writing without a firm idea of what is necessary to successfully create a Book Review on their own. No amount of exercises provided by *Write Source* detailing how to write a Book Review could make up for knowledge missed somewhere within the teaching/learning cycle. What follows is an example of how teachers could use both the detailed reading cycle and the teaching/learning cycle in regards to the *Bud, Not Buddy* Book Review.

Detailed reading

Preparation phase

In the Preparation phase for the Book Review, *Bud, Not Buddy*, the class begins by reading through the Book Review. Once the initial reading is over, common text features are identified. In the *Bud, Not Buddy* Book Review students may notice that the first paragraph introduces the title and author of the book, the main character of the book, and a quick summary about the main idea of the entire book. The summary in the first paragraph also contains a statement relating the book to everyday life.

The main body of *Bud, Not Buddy* is essentially a chronological retelling of the book. The teacher may point out that the beginning of the main body includes information about the setting of the book and the central conflict to the story. The rest of the main body describes what the main character, Bud, does to solve this conflict and the different types of situations he gets himself into along with the different types of people he meets along the way. The information contained in the main body is also relevant to the story as a whole with non-essential information left out. The end of the main body is where the main conflict in the story is solved.

In the last paragraph of the *Bud, Not Buddy* Book Review, teachers and students may discuss how the author has chosen to highlight his/her favorite part of the whole story and why the book is good. The last few sentences of the whole Book Review also revisit the main idea first introduced in the Context and why this might be important to note for the structure of the Book Review.

Identification phase

After identifying the main structure of the Book Review and seeing how the text is structured, students are now able to look at specific meanings at the sentence level. As identified earlier in the textual analysis, students might want to identify what words the writer used to represent the shifts in time from the story. They could also identify what types of Processes are used when the writer talks about Bud as he is central to the entire story. The teacher may also want to help students identify how the writer thematically develops the text, and what the thematic variations mean.

Elaboration phase

Now that students have gone through the preparation phase and identification phase when looking at the *Bud, Not Buddy* Book Review, they are now able to elaborate on any specific technical components. These may include making deliberate decisions on how to organize the Book Review, looking at better or more efficient ways of rendering a textual judgment, and further talking about the cohesive elements in an actual Book Review. There are other possibilities to consider in the detailed reading cycle of this particular Book Review, but regardless both the students and the teacher will be more knowledgeable about the genre as they enter into the teaching/learning cycle.

Teaching/learning cycle

Deconstruction

By following the detailed reading cycle, the teacher and students have completed an important part of the Deconstruction phase in the teaching/learning cycle. In the Deconstruction phase students and teachers also examine the specific field and context of the Book Review. Discussing why Book Reviews in general are important as well as what types of information are communicated in them would be essential for students to fully deconstruct a text. *Write Source* only includes two examples of Book Reviews for the entire unit. Students and teachers may want to look at numerous samples of Book Reviews and look at important issues of organization and information across a wide spectrum to see if there are repeating themes and ideas. It may also be important to see how Book Reviews are used not only in an academic setting, but also in out-of-school literacy settings as well in order to connect in- and out-of-school learning.

Joint Construction

While the *Bud, Not Buddy* Book Review is an excellent example, students may be more focused on the plot line information rather than the actual Book Review itself if they do not know the story. Students may also lose interest in writing the Book Review because *Bud, Not Buddy* holds little to no significance for them. This is where the power of shared experience and Joint Construction is found. For example, after reading a class novel together, teachers and students can use their combined knowledge not only to elaborate on the actual book itself, but also to discuss what important elements they would want to include in a Book Review. Comprehension of the book is strengthened in the process, as is the motivation to write the Book Review. Joint Construction also enables the teacher to provide more scaffolding on how to write a Book Review to the entire class more so than they would get if students jumped straight to the Individual Construction cycle.

Individual Construction

Once students reach this stage, they now have a stronger grasp of the Book Review genre through the discussions and experiences of detailed reading and the teaching/learning cycle. While it still may be necessary to provide scaffolding to students, just like sample exercises in *Write Source*, the scaffolding is only there to fill in gaps and not to force students to do something they already understand. In addition, students will already have a strong knowledge of what makes up a Book Review and may begin to explore the possibility of transforming the genre rather than just reproducing it like so many textbooks require.

Conclusion

As stated earlier, the purpose of the Book Review is to move students away from the informal and not as valued personal responses to more abstract ways of thinking. The problem, though, is that "without a language for discussing the ways texts are constructed, students are confined to discussing the details of story and character" (Christie & Derewianka, 2010, p. 67). It is also worth mentioning that educators may also need to spend time teaching their students how to read Book Reviews in order for them to be better prepared to actually write one. The textual analysis of *Bud, Not Buddy* provides further insight into the important elements of a Book Review in attempts to prepare writers to meaningfully evaluate texts.

What, then, is gained through examining the different language metafunctions, detailed reading, and the teaching/learning cycle? By providing students with the metalanguage necessary to deconstruct and reconstruct texts on their own, students can become more successful readers and writers once the scaffolding present in the teaching/learning cycle is taken away (Martin, 2006). Students will not only be required to write Book Reviews throughout their educational careers, but they will also be asked to reproduce many types of genre, year after year. As these genres grow increasingly complex, students will have gained the necessary skills and knowledge to navigate whatever new concepts are introduced and experiment along the way.

References

Christie, F., & Derewianka, B. (2010). *School discourse: Learning to write across the years of schooling*. London: Continuum.

Cope, B., & Kalantzis, M. (1993). Introduction: How a genre approach to literacy can transform the way writing is taught. In B. Cope & M. Kalantzis. (Eds.), *The powers of literacy: A genre approach to teaching writing* (pp. 1–21). Pittsburgh, PA: University of Pittsburgh Press.

Johns, A. (2008). Genre awareness for the novice academic student: An ongoing quest. *Language Teaching, 41*(2), 237–252. http://dx.doi.org/10.1017/S0261444807004892

Martin, J. R. (2006). Metadiscourse: Designing interaction in genre-based literacy programmes. In R. Whittaker, M. O'Donnell & A. McCabe (Eds.), *Language and literacy: Functional approaches* (pp. 95–122). London: Continuum.

Martin, J. R., & Rose, D. (2005). Designing literacy pedagogy: scaffolding democracy in the classroom. In R. Hasan, C. M. I. M. Matthiessen, & J. J. Webster (Eds.), *Continuing discourse on language: A functional perspective* (Vol. 1) (pp. 250–280). Oakville, CT: Equinox.

Martin, J. R., & Rose, D. (2008). *Genre relations: Mapping culture*. London: Equinox.

Rose, D., & Martin, J. R. (2012). *Learning to write, reading to learn: Genre, knowledge and pedagogy in the Sydney School*. Sheffield: Equinox.

Rothery, J., & Stenglin, M. (1997). Entertaining and instructing: Exploring experience through story. In In F. Christie & J. R. Martin (Eds.). *Genre and institutions: Social processes in the workplace and school* (pp. 231–263). London: Continuum.

Sebranek, P., Kemper, D., & Meyer, V. (2008) *Write source*. Wilmington, MA: Houghton Mifflin.

Appendix A

Theme // Rheme (marked themes are bolded)

CONTEXT

Bud, Not Buddy by Christopher Paul Curtis // is a story about a young boy finding people who care about him. Like all of us, Bud // knows that having people who care for you is a lucky thing. The "family" that Bud finds // has some of the same qualities that a lot of families have today. This story // shows that some members of a family may not be related, but they // still care for each other.

TEXT DESCRIPTION

When the story starts, // 10-year-old Bud lives with his mother in Flint, Michigan. It // is 1936, and the Great Depression // is making life hard for most people. Times // are very difficult, but they // become more difficult for Bud after his mother dies. She // never tells him who his father is. Bud // thinks a man named Herman E. Calloway may be his father because of five posters his mother has kept through the years. The posters // advertise a band named Herman E. Calloway and the Dusky Devastators of the Depression. Bud // sets out to find Herman E. Calloway.

Many things // happen to Bud as he searches. All of the situations that he comes across // show readers what the Great Depression was like. **For example**, // Bud spends time with other homeless people. He // tries to leap into a boxcar of a moving train to get to another city. He // also waits in food lines and eats at missions. We // see how strangers help each other and become like the extended families we have today.

When Bud finally reaches Grand Rapids, // he finds Calloway and tells him his story. Calloway // says he is not Bud's father. However, he // gives Bud jobs in exchange for room and board. Bud // doesn't unpack the few things he owns: an old blanket, five smooth rocks with letters and dots written on them, the five posters, and a picture of his mother. **Because Calloway is a grumpy, rather mean person**, // Bud thinks about moving on, but the band members // are good to Bud. **For one thing**, // they buy him an old saxophone. This // is one of the ways they show Bud they care. The band members // know each other's weaknesses and skills. They // are a family in many ways, and Bud // likes being part of their lives.

The five smooth rocks, not the posters, // turn out to be the key to Bud's identity. **When Bud discovers that Calloway has a collection of smooth stones in the glove compartment of his car**, // he tells Calloway, "I've got some of these, sir." Calloway // turns out to be his mother's father, not Bud's father, but this // makes Calloway his grandfather.

TEXT JUDGMENT

One of the best parts of the story // is when Bud gets his old blanket out and remakes his bed. Now he // knows this is the bed his mom slept in as a child. Readers // know now that he isn't going to leave. **Even though Bud never finds his father**, // he has found a "family" in the band members and a grouchy grandfather. Not all members of his family // are related by blood, but they // care for him as any family would.

Appendix B
Textual cohesion

Bud, Not Buddy by Christopher Paul Curtis is a story about a young boy finding people who care about him. Like all of us, Bud knows that having people who care for you is a lucky thing. The "family" that Bud finds has some of the same qualities that a lot of families have today. (This story) shows that some members of a **family** may not be related, but (they) still care for each other.

When the **story** starts, 10-year-old Bud lives with his mother in Flint, Michigan. (It) is 1936, and the Great Depression is making life hard for most people. **Times** are very difficult, but (they) become more difficult for Bud after his mother dies. She never tells him who his father is. Bud thinks a man named Herman E. Calloway may be his father because of five posters his mother has kept through the years. The posters advertise a band named Herman E. Calloway and the Dusky Devastators of the Depression. Bud sets out to find Herman E. Calloway.

Many things happen to **Bud** as he searches. All of the situations that (he) comes across show readers what the Great Depression was like. For example, Bud spends time with other homeless people. He tries to leap into a boxcar of a moving train to get to another city. He also waits in food lines and eats at missions. We see how strangers help each other and become like the extended families we have today.

When Bud finally reaches Grand Rapids, he finds Calloway and tells him his story. **Calloway** says he is not Bud's father. However, (he) gives Bud jobs in exchange for room and board. Bud doesn't unpack the few things he owns: an old blanket, five smooth rocks with letters and dots written on them, the five posters, and a picture of his mother. Because Calloway is a grumpy, rather mean person, Bud thinks about moving on, but the **band members** are good to Bud. For one thing, (they) **buy him an old saxophone**. (This) is one of the ways they show Bud they care. The **band members** know each other's weaknesses and skills. (They) are a family in many ways, and Bud likes being part of their lives.

The five smooth rocks, not the posters, turn out to be the key to Bud's identity. When Bud discovers that Calloway has a collection of smooth stones in the glove compartment of his car, he tells Calloway, "I've got some of these, sir." **Calloway turns out to be his mother's father**, not Bud's father, but (this) makes Calloway his grandfather.

One of the best parts of the story is when Bud gets his old blanket out and remakes his bed. Now he knows this is the bed his mom slept in as a child. Readers know now that he isn't going to leave. Even though Bud never finds his father, he has found a "family" in the band members and a grouchy grandfather. Not all **members of his family** are related by blood, but (they) care for him as any family would.

8 Filling in the gaps: genre as a scaffold to the text types of the Common Core State Standards

Michael Maune and Marshall Klassen

The Common Core State Standards (CCSS) are the newest set of educational standards based in the United States designed to ensure that all students are prepared for the challenges that await them in college and their careers. These standards also present to teachers a new challenge in that they must find the most effective ways to address the standards in their teaching. The English Language Arts (ELA) standards "insist that instruction in reading, writing, speaking, listening and language be a shared responsibility" (National Governors Association Center for Best Practices & Council of Chief State School Officers, 2010a, p. 4) for all teachers across grade levels and content areas. Therefore, all teachers will need to be able to teach writing regardless of their subjects, and will be expected to fulfill these standards of reading, writing, speaking, and listening even in areas where focus on language is often not directly addressed.

A close examination of the standards reveals several tools for teachers to use when implementing them in their classroom. The CCSS includes a compilation of student writing samples complete with "annotations to illustrate the criteria required" (NGA & CCSSO, 2010b, p. 2) to fulfill the standards in the three "text types"—argument, informative/explanatory, narrative—across different grades and subjects. These annotations reference and cite the student samples to display how each standard is being met and provide the context in which the text was written. However, some limitations of the annotations and the writing standards in general are the abstract nature of the expectations of the text types. In order to bridge the gap between the abstract standards and the specific language choices of the student texts, teachers need a more descriptive resource for teaching the language specific to each text type. Systemic functional linguistics (SFL) provides a scaffold to make explicit meaning making from the language choices that are inherent in the abstract expectations of each text type in the standards.

In order to demonstrate the scaffolding power of SFL, we conducted an analysis of the student samples using two frameworks: the CCSS and the SFL-based approach. SFL-based pedagogy has shown to be beneficial to students in making explicit the purpose behind language and the types of language that accomplish specific social processes (de Oliveira, 2011; Rose & Martin, 2012; Schleppegrell, 2004; Schleppegrell & de Oliveira, 2006). This chapter provides an overview of the writing standards in the CCSS, including the major organizing framework of *text types*. We then briefly introduce each of the student samples, describing their text type and genre characteristics. Next, we closely examine the samples and annotations in the CCSS, and then provide an SFL analysis of those same texts. Lastly, we propose how these two frameworks may be used together to create a more coherent whole that will be beneficial to both educators and students alike.

Overview of writing standards for CCSS

The CCSS Writing Standards use the concept of a *text type* as their primary organizational framework for setting out what students should know and be able to do when writing. As such, the writing expectations for students are tied to both the purpose of the text and the rhetorical and linguistic conventions that realize each text type. The three text types, as mentioned above, include argument, informative/explanatory, and narrative. Due to space constraints, we will focus only on informative/explanatory and narrative. The standards for each text type begin at kindergarten and become increasingly more complex as the students develop. This means that students begin learning all the text types from the first year in school and build on that base as they develop. More complex concepts at higher grades are generally realized by more complex language and more detailed specifications in the standards. It is helpful to think of the Writing Standards as a continuum of expectations, where students build on a foundation for each text type throughout their scholastic career, culminating in an understanding of a variety of genres, writing purposes, and rhetorical and linguistic tools available for composing in each text type.

The informative/explanatory text type's purpose is "to increase readers' knowledge of a subject, to help readers better understand a procedure or process, or to provide readers with an enhanced comprehension of a concept" (NGA & CCSSO, 2010c, p. 23). In order to accomplish this, students are expected to draw from primary and secondary sources as a basis of knowledge. The standards list a variety of techniques students should use to meet this goal. Interestingly, the CCSS explicitly mentions genre in its definition of informative/explanatory text type:

> informative/explanatory writing includes a wide array of genres, including academic genres such as literary analyses, scientific and historical reports, summaries, and précis writing as well as forms of workplace and functional writing such as instructions, manuals, memos, reports, applications, and résumés. (NGA & CCSSO, 2010c, p. 23)

As students progress in grade level they are expected to "expand their repertoire of … genres" (p. 23). This suggests that text types contain different kinds of genres; in other words, genres are more specific kinds of texts, while text types denote a broader way of thinking about texts. In this way, text types are similar to macro-genres or families of genres (Martin & Rose, 2008). This distinction becomes important when analyzing student texts because a genre approach will highlight more detailed purposes and linguistic constructions than the broader outlook that text type analysis offers. Other implications for this distinction will be discussed in the latter part of this chapter.

The narrative text type is also defined by its purpose(s), "to inform, instruct, persuade, or entertain" (NGA & CCSSO, 2010c, p. 23). This text type is given the greatest amount of freedom, as students are to fulfill these purposes through the use of different forms of narrative, and over time must provide various details (visual, situational, character actions, interior monologue, etc.) and be comfortable using narrative across content areas, where applicable. Although these text types are described and connected to their purposes, the CCSS do include a caveat that gives examples of texts that "blend types" and goes on to state that "effective student writing can also cross the boundaries of type" and cites an example in Appendix C, which is a compendium of exemplary student texts.

The sample student texts examined in this chapter are included in Appendix C of the CCSS and correspond to two different text types. We have selected two eighth grade student texts in order to focus on one particular stage in the continuum of expectations. We selected narrative and informative/explanatory text types as the focus of our analysis because they show a broader range of linguistic and genre features that students need to know and teachers need to teach. Furthermore, Appendix C only provides narrative student texts up to eighth grade; the high school standards emphasize more informative/ explanatory and argument writing over narrative. The standards for the two text types at the seventh and eighth grade are moderately complex and are reproduced below in Figure 8.1 and Figure 8.2. We will provide a brief overview of the standards at this general grade level.

In middle school, students are expected to become familiar with the concept of *cohesion* and begin developing a "formal style" (NGA & CCSSO, 2010a, p. 42) as a general property of good writing in the informative/explanatory and argument text types, while in narrative, students begin to manipulate a

Grade 7 students:	Grade 8 students:
2. Write informative/explanatory texts to examine a topic and convey ideas, concepts, and information through the selection, organization, and analysis of relevant content. a. Introduce a topic clearly, previewing what is to follow; organize ideas, concepts, and information, using strategies such as definition, classification, comparison/contrast, and cause/effect; include formatting (e.g., headings), graphics (e.g., charts, tables), and multimedia when useful to aiding comprehension. b. Develop the topic with relevant facts, definitions, concrete details, quotations, or other information and examples. c. Use appropriate transitions to create cohesion and clarify the relationships among ideas and concepts. d. Use precise language and domain-specific vocabulary to inform about or explain the topic. e. Establish and maintain a formal style. f. Provide a concluding statement or section that follows from and supports the information or explanation presented.	2. Write informative/explanatory texts to examine a topic and convey ideas, concepts, and information through the selection, organization, and analysis of relevant content. a. Introduce a topic clearly, previewing what is to follow; organize ideas, concepts, and information into broader categories; include formatting (e.g., headings), graphics (e.g., charts, tables), and multimedia when useful to aiding comprehension. b. Develop the topic with relevant, well-chosen facts, definitions, concrete details, quotations, or other information and examples. c. Use appropriate and varied transitions to create cohesion and clarify the relationships among ideas and concepts. d. Use precise language and domain-specific vocabulary to inform about or explain the topic. e. Establish and maintain a formal style. f. Provide a concluding statement or section that follows from and supports the information or explanation presented.

Figure 8.1. Informative/Explanatory Writing for Common Core State Standards for Grade 7 & 8, 2010, p. 42

Grade 7 students:	Grade 8 students:
3. Write narratives to develop real or imagined experiences or events using effective technique, relevant descriptive details, and well-structured event sequences. a. Engage and orient the reader by establishing a context and point of view and introducing a narrator and/or characters; organize an event sequence that unfolds naturally and logically. b. Use narrative techniques, such as dialogue, pacing, and description, to develop experiences, events, and/or characters. c. Use a variety of transition words, phrases, and clauses to convey sequence and signal shifts from one time frame or setting to another. d. Use precise words and phrases, relevant descriptive detail, and sensory language to capture the action and convey experiences and events. e. Provide a conclusion that follows from and reflects on the narrated experiences or events.	3. Write narratives to develop real or imagined experiences or events using effective technique, relevant descriptive details, and well-structured event sequences. a. Engage and orient the reader by establishing a context and point of view and introducing a narrator and/or characters; organize an event sequence that unfolds naturally and logically. b. Use narrative techniques, such as dialogue, pacing, description, and reflection, to develop experiences, events, and/or characters. c. Use a variety of transition words, phrases, and clauses to convey sequence, signal shifts from one time frame or setting to another, and show the relationships among experiences and events. d. Use precise words and phrases, relevant descriptive detail, and sensory language to capture the action and convey experiences and events. e. Provide a conclusion that follows from and reflects on the narrated experiences or events.

Figure 8.2. Narrative Writing for Common Core State Standards for Grade 7 & 8, 2010, p. 43

sequence of events. *Claims* and *evidence* become part of the rhetorical resources available in the argument text type, while in the narrative text type, students add to their competence the concepts of *point of view* and *context*. Students also learn to provide a preview of their ideas in their introductions when writing in the informative/explanatory text type. Narratives also gain the resource of *reflection* as a possible technique for developing and concluding a story; students are also expected to use precise details to "capture the action" (NGA & CCSSO, 2010a, p. 43) of an event. In reviewing these grade level standards, the general development of the writing expectations is realized through increasingly abstract lexical choices such as *cohesion*, *evidence*, and *reflection*. Also noteworthy is the introduction of "formal style" which students will be expected to produce in the informative/explanatory and argument text types.

These linguistic choices in the standards may reflect the beginning development of abstract thought in the middle school grades (Brown & Knowles, 2007; Christie & Derewianka, 2008). Students are expected to understand abstract concepts like *cohesion* and be able to do complex tasks like form an argumentative *claim* and support it with *evidence* (NGA & CCSSO, 2010a). In some parts of the standards, certain linguistic constructions are specified as being useful in helping create these abstractions; for example, the standards advocate the use of "transition words" (p. 42), the use of quotations to develop a topic (p. 42), or dialogue to develop characters and events. However, in other parts, such as the standard addressing a "formal style," there is no description of a formal style or its purpose.

Student sample texts and analysis

The sample texts selected for analysis were included in the standards to "illustrate the criteria required to meet the CCSS for particular types of writing … in a given grade" (NGA & CCSSO, 2010b, p. 2). Each of the samples exhibits "at least the level of quality required to meet the Writing Standards for that grade" (p. 2). The samples from Appendix C are taken from assignments students completed in-class, for homework, as part of their classroom assessments, or as research projects. The two sample texts analyzed here are from grade 8.

The first text, "Miss Sadie" (NGA & CCSSO, 2010b, pp. 52–56), meets the expectations of the narrative text type. The second text, "The Old Man and the Sea" (pp. 49–51), fits the description of the informative/explanatory text type. The SFL analysis of these sample texts, revealed that "Miss Sadie" was an example of the Personal Narrative genre and the "The Old Man and the Sea" was a Character Analysis genre (Christie and Derewianka, 2008; Martin & Rose, 2008).

For the purpose of this analysis, we analyze the two genres, Personal Narrative ("Miss Sadie") and Character Analysis ("The Old Man and the Sea"), using the Appraisal system. Appraisal resources are language choices used to express emotions and to evaluate things, people, and processes. These resources include Judgment, Appreciation, and Affect. Judgment refers to evaluation of characters and their conduct based on ethical principles. Appreciation is used to "evaluate the worth and quality of things and processes," and Affect is used to express emotional reaction (Christie & Derewianka, 2008, pp. 15–16). These Appraisal resources mark important characteristics of the two genres we examined and help distinguish the genres from each other and from other genres. They help realize the unique social purpose of each genre through linking the language resources to the emotional/evaluative goals of each genre.

CCSS analysis of the narrative text

The Personal Narrative genre is defined in SFL as containing an orienting stage, a temporal sequence event where a complication (or disrupting event) is introduced, and closure or resolution where the complication is "solved" and may offer commentary at the end. Thus the schematic structure of the genre can be described: Orientation ^ Complication ^ Evaluation ^ Resolution ^ (Coda). Personal Narratives are characterized by the usage of personal pronouns (Christie & Derewianka, 2008).

The text sample entitled "Miss Sadie" was a Narrative written to fulfill an assignment where the students were asked to introduce a "special person" to readers, and were "advised" to reveal the personal quality of the relationship they shared with that "special person." This student had "borrowed ideas" from a fictional piece that she had read. The CCSS for grade 8 Narratives can be seen in Figure 8.1 above (NGA & CCSSO, 2010b, p. 52).

MISS SADIE[1]
APPRAISAL ANALYSIS
Judgment in *italics*, Appreciation is <u>underlined</u>, Affect in **bold**

ABSTRACT (Orientation)
(1) Miss Sadie no longer sits in her rocking chair on her porch on summer days. (2) But I still can see her, the old chair squeaking with every sway of the big, brown body. (3) Her summer dresses stained from cooking her <u>sweet</u> smelling kitchen. (4) I see her gray hair pulled back in that <u>awful</u> yellow banana clip. (5) Most of all, I hear that voice. (6) *So full of character and wisdom.*

ORIENTATION
(7) I used to bring Miss Johnson cookies every summer day of 1988. (8) **I miss the days** here I would sit on that <u>shabby old</u> porch_and listen to her stories, "Melissa!" (9) She would holler. (10) "What 'chu doin' here? Come see me and my **poor** self, have ya?"

(11) She once told me of her grandmother who <u>escaped</u> slavery, back when white men could only do anything, she would say. (12) Her grandma ran for miles without food or water. (13) It

[1] Text found in Common Core State Standards Appendix C, pp. 52–54.

wasn't too long before her master came looking for her and took her home to whip her. (14) I thought of how Blacks are treated today. (15) **I sighed**. (16) She would sing in her soulful, blaring voice, old negro hymns passed down from her mother and grandmother. (17) I would sit there in **amazement**.

(18) Once, Jimmy Taylor came walking by us yellin, "Melissa! Whattaya want with that *old, fat, Black lady,* anyways?"

(19) Before I could **retaliate**, Miss Johnson said to me, "Now you mustn't. (20) We **must feel sorry** for that *terrible child.* (21) His mother must have done gone and not taught him no manners!" (22) She **actually** wanted me **to bow my head and pray for him**. (23) (Even though I went to his house and **punched him out** the next day.)

(24) My friends would **tease me** for spending the whole summer with Sadie Johnson, *"The cuckoo of Connecticut"* they called her. (25) But I'm **so very glad** I did. (26) She taught me then, **to not care what other people thought**. (27) I learned that I could be friends with someone generations apart from my own.

COMPLICATION

(28) My visits became less frequent when school started. (29) I had **other things** to think about. (30) Boys, clothes, grades. You know, real important stuff.

(31) One day I was thinking, I haven't seen Miss Sadie in a while. (32) So after school I trotted up to her house amidst the twisting, autumn leaves.

(33) I rang her bell. (34) The door cracked open and the woman adjusted her glasses. (34) "May I help you?"

(35) "Miss Sadie, it's me, Melissa."

(36) "I-I" she'd stuttered. "I don't remember", she said and shut the door. (37) I heard crying. (38) I rang the door again and she screamed, "Please leave!" in a scared, confused voice.

(39) I went home **bewildered** and my mother told me to stop bothering Miss_Sadie. (40) I said I wasn't bothering her. (41) Mama said, "Miss Johnson has a disease. Alzheimer's disease. (42) It makes her forget things … people, family even. (43) And so, I don't want you over there anymore, you hear?"

EVALUATION

(44) Then, I didn't realize or comprehend how someone *so special* to you could forget your own existence when you'd shared a summer so special and vivid in your mind.

RESOLUTION

(45) That Christmas, I went to bring Miss Johnson cookies. (46) She wasn't there. (47) I learned from a family member that she was in the hospital and that she'd die very soon. (48) As the woman, a daughter maybe, spoke, **my heart broke**.

(49) "Well, you make sure she gets these cookies," I said, **my voice cracking and tears welling in my eyes**.

CODA (50) Today, I've learned to **love** old people. (51) For their *innocence*, for their knowledge, I've learned to always treat people with **kindness**, *no matter how cruel* they may seem. (52) But mainly I've learned that you must <u>cherish</u> the time spent with a person. (53) And memories are <u>very valuable.</u> (54) Because Miss Sadie no longer sits in her rocking chair on her porch on summer days. (55) I'm **glad** that I can still see her.

This student fulfills the standards by: "engaging and orienting the reader by establishing a context and introducing a narrator and characters" (8.W.3a). This is done by immediately entering the storyline and "backfilling information" about the setting (sentence 8: *shabby old porch*), their experience with Miss Sadie (sentences 8, 7: *listen to her stories*, *used to bring her cookies*) (NGA & CCSSO, 2010b, p. 55). The writer introduces these elements in a sequence appropriate for reflection (8.W.3a), where they introduce the present situation (sentence 1: *Miss Sadie no longer sits ...*) and engage in reflection describing Miss Sadie (sentences 2, 3: *big, brown body*, *summer dresses*).

The standard 8.W.3b is fulfilled by the reflection the writer engages in throughout the text (sentence 24: *spending the whole summer with Sadie ...*), the dialogue with Miss Sadie that creates tension, and the reports of internal thoughts and reactions of the characters in the story. The use of transition words conveying sequences throughout the story fulfills the standards in 8.W.3c and is listed in the Appendix C annotations, although little detail is given as to how these convey sequence or show relationships amongst the events in the story. Similarly in 8.W.3d, "precise words and phrases," "descriptive details," and "sensory language to capture the action" are cited from the text, but there are no explanations as to how the student accomplishes this. The conclusion is illustrated by the return to the beginning of the Narrative (sentence 54: *Miss Sadie no longer sits ...*), and reflects on the importance of their memories (sentence 55: *I'm glad that I can still see her*), fulfilling 8.W.3e. This text demonstrates "good command of the conventions of standard written English" and makes note that the usage of fragments in the story are for stylistic purposes (sentence 3: *Her summer dresses stained from cooking*).

The annotations for this sample text illustrate how each standard is fulfilled citing specific examples from the text, and give descriptions about which parts fulfill which standard, but do not give extensive detail into the type of language that should be used, for example adjectives or temporal words. The standards do detail the context (8.W.3a) that has been established through "skillfully backfilling information" about Miss Sadie (NGA & CCSSO,

2010b, p. 55). Furthermore, they recognize the uniqueness of the event sequence that should be "natural and logical," where this writer begins their reflection in the present time frame (8.W.3b). For standard 8.W.3.c, however, the Narrative techniques listed are simply cited as reflection, but no mention is made of the type of language that is necessary in reflecting on a past experience. Similarly, the standard "develop experiences" is fulfilled by the usage of "tension" and "reporting internal thoughts and reactions," but again, no mention of the type of language necessary to develop these techniques is made explicit in the annotations (NGA & CCSSO, 2010b, p. 55). The use of transition words (8.W.3d) are made explicit in the annotations (sentences 1, 2, 7: *no longer*, *still*, *used to*); however, there is no description in the next section about what makes the "precise words" and "relevant descriptive details and sensory language" able to "capture the action" of the story (p. 55).

These annotations are to be read and studied by teachers who are highly qualified professionals with experience teaching their students. These teachers will be able to create appropriate lessons for students who already have the benefit of being well-read in the genres of English and knowledge of how language works across genres. For those students without this implicit knowledge of how language accomplishes these goals, be they novice students or English language learners, these annotations, no matter how the teacher presents the knowledge, may be confusing to the students who would greatly benefit from learning *how* the language accomplishes these goals in an explicit way. In the next section, we will show how an SFL analysis may help teachers to bridge the linguistic gap left by the CCSS.

Bridging the gap: SFL analysis of narrative text

The SFL analysis of this sample text shows us many of the same elements that compose this genre also fulfill the CCSS standards. SFL characterizes this as a "Personal Narrative" due to the usage of personal pronouns throughout the text. The Narrative genre follows stages of Orientation, Complication, Evaluation, and Resolution. The "'point' of a Narrative is to [show] how the protagonists resolve a complication in their lives, once they have evaluated the complicating action with some type of attitude" (Martin & Rose, 2008). This corresponds with CCSS 8.W.3a and e, which establish orientation and conclusions, but do not specifically highlight the need to "resolve conflict."

The Orientation stage introduces Miss Sadie and her characteristics, using Appreciative language such as her "*soulful, blaring* voice," "gray hair pulled back in that *awful* yellow banana clip," (sentences 16, 4) which orients the reader by establishing a context and developing characters (8.W.3a and b). The Complication stage is introduced by the usage of nominalization of "My visits" (sentence 28), summarizing the entirety of the past two paragraphs and providing a temporal transition to continue to the Complication, "One day I was thinking, I haven't seen Miss Sadie in a while"(sentence 31). Temporal words and phrases are featured throughout the text—"Miss Sadie no longer …," "I used to …," "Once …," "Today …" (sentences 1, 7, 18, 50)—which orients the reader to the storyteller's time frame.

The Complication stage provides the greatest challenge to writers due to the freedom available as well as the patterns of evaluative language and/or reflective language involved. This language is critical in "establishing a context," "developing experiences and/or characters," "conveying sequence," and "us(ing) … words and … details … to capture the action" (8.W.3a, b, c, d). The evaluative language is critical to a successful Narrative, which conveys the point of the story (Christie & Derewianka, 2008).

The Evaluation stage uses evaluative language to "convey experiences and events" and "provide a conclusion" (8.W.3d, e). The writer uses phrases like "I went home **bewildered**", "someone *so special*," "**my voice cracking and tears welling in my eyes**," and "memories are <u>very valuable</u>" (sentences 39, 44, 49, 53) to emphasize the purpose of the story—that the writer had learned about the value of life and of the fragility and beauty of friendship across generations through this language (NGA & CCSSO, 2010b, p. 55).

The SFL analysis of this text is mostly concerned with the stages that characterize this genre and the language used that establishes context, characters, experiences, and reflection. The analysis shows that the Orientation stage uses language to establish context by using temporal language to set the time frame, Appreciation to develop the character and relationship between characters, and Judgment to show the strength of the connection they shared. The Complication stage also uses temporal words and phrases along with evaluative language to illustrate the introduction of the Complication and how it affects the characters, further developing experiences, with the use of Affect to convey this. The reflection shows that evaluative language is used to show what the "point" of the story was, to show that the writer had gained and learned something from the story.

The genre approach is mostly concerned with how the language is being used in the story and how it builds up the experiences that are being described. In this approach, for example, the teacher would analyze the text beforehand, and explain to the students what each bit of descriptive language is doing and how it establishes context, character development, experiences, etc. An alternate reconstruction using different language which still establishes the same experiences would help scaffold independent construction of students' writing, which fulfills the CCSS standards while making explicit the language that does so.

CCSS analysis of informative/explanatory text

The Character Analysis genre gives a broad overview of a character or characters in one story and often makes connections and reflections about life in general, drawing logical connections from the characters to reality. The schematic structure of the genre can be described: Character Presentation ^ Character Description ^ Character Judgment. Features of these texts involve Appreciation of the situations that they find themselves in and evaluations made, and Judgment about their ethical principles and how they conduct their lives. This genre has students use grammar differently to distance themselves from the text and use "showing" verbs in order to reveal the nature of the characters through their actions (Christie & Derewianka, 2008).

In "The Old Man and the Sea," the student writer demonstrates command of the informative/explanatory text type at the grade 8 level during a homework assignment for English class. The annotations provided in Appendix C illustrate how the student fulfills many of the grade level standards for the text type throughout the essay. Most significantly, the student shows considerable competence at developing a thesis through examples.

The Old Man and the Sea[3]
INTERPERSONAL AND TEXTUAL ANALYSIS
Judgment in *italics*, Appreciation is underlined, Affect in **bold**

Character Presentation

(1) In the book The Old Man and the Sea, Ernest Hemingway tells the story of an *old Cuban fisherman* named Santiago who, *considered by the villagers to be the worst type of unlucky*, is still *determined to win* a battle against a giant Marlin of the coast of Cuba. (2) *Santiago succeeds*, but his successes do not come without great hardship and struggle. (3) He spends three days being dragged in his skiff by the enormous marlin with minimal food and water, all the while enduring acute physical pain, tiredness, **and an unending loneliness** due to the absence of his young friend, Manolin. (4) It is only after Santiago's prize fish is completely devoured by sharks that he returns home to the *village scorners* and the safety of Manolin's trust. (5) As his suffering and loss compound, we can see that Hemingway's quote *"a man can be destroyed but not defeated"* offers a key insight into Santiago's life.

Character Description

(6) As the story begins, we learn that Santiago has gone eighty-four days straight without catching a fish. (7) Young Manolin's parents will no longer allow the two to fish together, for they do not want their son being exposed any more to this *type of failure*. (8) **Santiago and**

[3] Text found in Common Core State Standards Appendix C, pp. 49-51.

Manolin are deeply saddened by this news, but Santiago *does not let* the loss of his friend or *the defeat that others see him suffering* keep him off the sea. (9) Rather, with bright and shining eyes he thinks "maybe today. (10) Every day is a new day" (pg. 32), and prepares to catch the biggest fish of his life. (11) This shows that even though almost all of Santiago's acquaintances **feel that his fishing career is over, he sees it about to reach its all time high**. (12) Though he knows he is physically older and weaker than most of his fellow fishermen, *he refuses to let their opinions and stereotypes destroy his confidence and determination.*

(13) As the story progresses, Hemingway presents an even more vivid picture of *Santiago refusing to be destroyed by the forces that threaten to defeat him.* (14) Even after he accomplishes the difficult task of hooking the giant Marlin, he finds his skiff being dragged by the fish for over two days. (15) Living in the small boat is no easy task for Santiago, and soon injury and suffering seem to take over his entire body. (16) His back is sore from sitting so long against the stiff wood, his face is cut from fishing hooks, his shoulders ache, and his eyes have trouble focusing. (17) Most difficult to endure though is the terrible condition in which he finds his hands. (18) The left one is weakened from a period of being tightly cramped, and both are extremely mutilated from the burn of the moving fishing line. (19) It would have been so much easier for Santiago to simply give up and release the fish, yet he knows that if he endures a little longer, victory will be his. (20) Even when it seems he has no effort left, *Santiago promises himself "I'll try it again."* (pg. 93) (21) *This is Santiago's real inner determination coming through.* (22) He has encountered so many obstacles during the past few days, yet he will not let them *defeat his dream of killing the fish.* (23) There is no outside force promising a splendid reward if he succeeds, only those that threaten to ridicule him if he is destroyed. (24) *Santiago is working solely on his own desire to fulfill his dream and prove to himself that, although his struggles may cost him his life, he can accomplish even the seemingly impossible.*

After three long days and nights, Santiago's determination pays off, and at last he manages to catch and kill the Marlin. (25) It is only a very short time that he has to **relish in his triumph** though, for a few hours later vicious sharks begin to destroy the carcass of the great fish. (26) For hours, Santiago manages to ward them of, *but this time it is not he who wins the final battle.* (27) **Spirits low** and pain at an all time high, Santiago returns to the village, towing behind him only the bare skeleton of a treasure that once was. (28) *It seems as though Santiago is ready to just curl up and die, and indeed he has reason to feel this way.* (29) Yet as he rests alone and talks with Manolin, we see *a hint of Santiago's determination, that has characterized his personality throughout the entire story, begin to shine through.* (30) Upon reaching home, he begins to make plans with Manolin about future adventures they will have together. (31) Hemingway tells us that Santiago, in his youth, **had loved to watch** the majestic lions along his home on a white sand beach in Africa, and he still returns to those dreams when **searching for contentment**. (32) That night, as Santiago drifts off to sleep, Hemingway tells that he was indeed "dreaming about the lions." (pg. 127) (33) *This is perhaps the truest test of how much courage and determination a person has.* (34) If even when they have suffered the biggest defeat of their life, they are able to look to the future and realize the wonderful things they still possess. (35) *Though the forces of nature and time destroyed Santiago's prize fish, he refuses to let that fact ruin the rest of his life. No one can take away his love for Manolin or memories of what once was, and because of this, no one can ever truly defeat Santiago.*

Character Judgment

(36) In conclusion, throughout the entire story The Old Man and the Sea, *Santiago refuses to*

surrender to the forces working against him. (37) *He ignores the comments of those who think he is unlucky, endures great physical pain, and rises up from the depths of sorrow over the lost Marlin to find happiness in what he does possess.* (38) *Hemingway's quote "a man can be destroyed but not defeated" truly does display the amount of determination that Santiago shows throughout his life.*

The student explains their thesis through a quote from Hemingway, explaining: "As his suffering and loss compound, we can see that Hemingway's quote 'a man can be destroyed but not defeated' offers a key insight into Santiago's life" (NGA & CCSSO, 2010b, p. 50). This particular sentence helps introduce the main topic of determination in the face of adversity, thus fulfilling standard 8.W.2a. The annotations then explain that each of the following paragraphs in the text provide "extended examples" of Santiago's suffering and determination, citing multiple sentences from the student writing. This paragraph structure choice of the student fulfills 8.W.2b, which expects students to "organize ideas, concepts, and information into broader categories". The specific "categories" stipulated by the standard might be the "examples of Santiago's struggle and determination". Each paragraph could then be seen as "information" conveying these "examples." The annotations do not explicitly connect the text to the abstractions in standard, like "categories" or "concepts," and thus the analysis here is at best an inference.

The next standard addressed, 8.W.2b, lists a number of rhetorical and linguistic structures as tools in "developing a topic." The annotations then specify sentences where the student uses "concrete details," "quotations," and "examples." However, the specific connection between these selections from the text and the abstract standard is not explicitly addressed. The relationship might be inferred that these details and quotations further build the topic of Santiago's suffering and determination. The same issue appears in the annotations for standard 8.W.2d, which expects students to "use precise language and domain-specific vocabulary to inform about or explain the topic". The annotations list selections from the text, such as "minimal food and water … acute physical pain … eighty-four days straight without catching a fish … only the bare skeleton" as examples of precise language, do not show how these examples develop the topic.

Lastly, the annotations address standard 8.W.2e, which states that students should "establish and maintain a formal style". One example of this formal style is shown in the first sentence of the essay: "In the book The Old Man and the Sea, Ernest Hemingway tells the story of an old Cuban fisherman named Santiago who, considered by the villagers to be the worst type of unlucky, is still determined to win a battle against a giant Marlin off the coast of Cuba".

Unfortunately, the annotations do not provide an explanation for why this selection fulfills the standard; the annotation simply denotes that the standard is fulfilled in this sentence. What seems left implicit is the nature of a "formal style," which may be problematic for writers who have no prior knowledge of such a style. This problem is exacerbated by the fact that the formal style standard is first introduced in the seventh grade—that is, it is a concept that has no prior referent in the continuum. While the student sample texts show what the style looks like, it is unclear what features in the sample make it "formal" and why formality is important.

Bridging the gap: SFL analysis of the informative/explanatory text

Analyzing the text from a genre perspective can show the function of certain language choices in the student text and provide more concrete concepts and structures to serve as a scaffold to the more general abstraction of the informative/explanatory text type and its corresponding standards. From an SFL perspective, "The Old Man and the Sea" falls into a family of Response Genres common in ELA because they are used to respond to literature. The specific genre of Character Analysis aims to develop a Judgment of a character based on an Appreciation of the circumstances the character encounters. In order to accomplish this goal, the genre utilizes three stages: Character Presentation, where the character is introduced; Character Description, where the character's circumstances are presented and evaluated; and Character Judgment, where the character is evaluated morally. The student text fulfills this genre expectation in a variety of ways, mainly through utilizing resources of Appraisal associated with each stage of the genre.

In the first paragraph, the student presents the character of Santiago through a series of sentences that describe Santiago's journey in the novella. In the last sentence of the paragraph, the writer creates a thesis statement that thematically ties the text together cohesively: "As his suffering and loss compound, we can see that Hemingway's quote '*a man can be destroyed but not defeated*' offers a key insight into Santiago's life" (sentence 5). The student author uses Appraisal abstractions like "suffering" and "loss" to convey the conditions of Santiago's life. The fact that the thesis statement is a dependent clause suggests the student is reasoning across clauses, contending that the "suffering" and "loss" may lead to some purpose. The use of Appraisal resources later in this sentence foreground and foreshadow Character Judgment as the primary goal of the text. The student links the moral Judgment invoked in the words "destroyed but not defeated" to Santiago through the Process "offers." In this thesis statement, the writer's goal becomes clear: the student intends to show how Santiago's life reveals some "ethical principles of living" (Christie & Derewianka, 2008). The presence of the thesis statement at the end of this paragraph also marks the end of the Character Presentation stage and the beginning of the Character Description.

In the Character Description, the student begins with a topic sentence that describes the circumstances of Santiago's suffering. "As the story begins, we learn that Santiago has gone eighty-four days straight without catching a fish" (sentence 6). The student then uses attitudinal lexis, focusing on Appreciation, to develop an evaluation of Santiago's circumstances: "loss of his friend, difficult task, injury and suffering, terrible condition, extremely mutilated" (sentences 8, 14, 15, 17, 18). These word choices convey the student writer's Appreciation of the circumstances experienced by Santiago. Yet Santiago's responses to these circumstances become the basis for the writer's Judgment of him, which begins in the Character description with sentences like: "Most difficult to endure though is the terrible condition in which he finds his hands ... Even when it seems he has no effort left, *Santiago promises himself 'I'll try it again.'* (pg. 93) This is Santiago's real inner determination coming through" (sentences 17, 20, 21). In this line of reasoning, the student writer Appreciates the character's condition ("terrible condition" of his hands) and then links Santiago's response ("I'll try again") to his Judgment of the Character ("Santiago's real inner determination").

The writer summarizes his/her Character Judgment in the final paragraph that begins: "In conclusion, throughout the entire story The Old Man and the Sea, *Santiago refuses to surrender to the forces working against him*" (sentence 36). The author thus renders a Judgment of Santiago as having determination in the face of adversity through the phrase "refuses to surrender to the forces working against him."

The genre analysis shows the various Appraisal resources the student uses to accomplish the specific goal of showing how Santiago's life and circumstances can reveal some ethical principle, like determination. In comparison to the CCSS annotation, the genre analysis allows students to see a specific purpose for a text, rather than a general one like "inform," and provides a framework of stages that are commonly used to accomplish this goal. Combining the rhetorical resources of the CCSS with the Appraisal resources of SFL provides students with a variety of tools for understanding the text; however, the SFL resources more closely link the language with a specific goal defined by the genre, whereas rhetorical devices like "examples" and "precise language" are general enough to be used for multiple purposes.

General comparison across approaches and implications

In a comparative analysis of the CCSS annotations and SFL analysis, the common goal of linking language with function is evident in both conceptual systems. For example, the CCSS expects students to use transition words (language) to create cohesion in a text (function) and to use details, examples, and facts (language) to develop a topic (function). Similarly, SFL predicts writers of Character Analyses will use Appraisal resources of Judgment (language) to convey an ethical position on a person through Appreciation of the person's circumstances and actions (function). Both the CCSS and SFL see language as an activity of relating form with function; Martin & Rose's definition of genre seems to overlap well with the text types of the CCSS: "We characterize genres as staged, goal-oriented, social processes" (2008, p. 6). Certainly the text types have in common with SFL's genres the notion of being goal oriented. However, the stages that characterize genres and their corresponding social processes are unique to SFL and bring to our understanding of text discrete ways to teach students organizational strategies of text structures that accomplish some social purpose, thus helping them understand how specific language forms accomplish specific social functions.

The narrative text type in the CCSS gives a detailed outline for teachers to offer their students, but offer little explicit instruction as to how to accomplish the standards listed, such as "engage and orient the reader" or "use narrative techniques … to develop experiences, events and/or characters." Through the additional lens of SFL, we can see through the Orientation, Complication, Evaluation, and Resolution stages how each uses the resources of Appraisal to accomplish the expectations of the Personal Narrative genre of SFL, and the narrative text type in the CCSS. The marriage of these frameworks can give teachers the resources to show students how to use language to accomplish these expectations and equip them with the skills to become better writers.

When addressing abstract and general concepts in the CCSS, like "Establish and maintain a formal style" (8.W.2e), research in SFL can provide discrete scaffolds for teachers to use. In the example of "formal style," the teacher might employ the research of Schleppegrell (2004) to address the standard. Schleppegrell uses the resources of SFL to describe the discrete characteristics of academic register—the "formal style" expected of students and the main register employed in informative/explanatory text types. Among these features are the reliance on Material, Relational, and Existential Processes to convey abstract meanings, Declarative mood and Median modality to articulate debatable ideas and arguments, and Grammatical Metaphor to condense complex Processes, Participants, and Circumstances into more abstract terms. These specific linguistic functional concepts construct the idea of "formal style" so that teachers might support student learning of the standard.

In much the same way, the stages of genres can be used as discrete scaffolds for teaching the concepts of text types. More significantly, where the

CCSS render general functions for linguistic forms, like "Develop a topic with relevant facts, definitions, concrete details, quotations, or other information and examples" (8.W.2b), the stages of genres can provide specific functions that fit within the general function expected by the CCSS. For 8.W.2b, a teacher might use a Character Analysis as a scaffolding genre to help students understand and practice the standard. The Character Analysis has as its goal the description of a character in order to highlight some moral principle for living illustrated by the character's life. This fits within the 8.W.2 general standard for informative/explanatory texts. The topic is introduced (8.W.2a) through the thesis statement of the Character Presentation, where the author introduces the character through generalizations and offers a Judgment in the thesis. The topic is developed (8.W.2b) in the Character Description, where the writer describes the character using Appreciation resources to evaluate the character's circumstances and actions—which leads to ethical Judgments of the character. All throughout, the student might use scaffolds based on academic register to create a formal style (8.W.2e). And lastly, the student would conclude (8.W.2f) with the Character Judgment stage, offering a lesson based on the character's life. This genre's schematic structure would provide the teacher and student substantial support for learning the writing standards for the text type through the detailed metalanguage resources of SFL.

The genre approach concerns itself with how the language makes meaning throughout the text. In distinguishing itself from a genre approach, an analysis of the exemplar annotations in Appendix C reveals that the CCSS identify general linguistic and rhetorical constructions and link them to some function in the standard. However, the annotations do not consistently *explain* the nature of the link between the phrase and the abstract function. The specific instantiations of these text types as realized by the student sample may show *what* the text type looks like and even *what* specific abstract standards might look like when fulfilled, but the annotations do not always clearly explain *why* or *how* specific selections fulfill the standards. Thus, a gap exists between the level of abstraction in the standards and the level of specificity inherent in the student text. However, by adapting an SFL approach in the classroom, teachers can offer students resources to analyze texts by identifying language features, stages, and specific linguistic phrases to fulfill the expectations of the CCSS. Teachers will be better equipped to identify the features that characterize each text type for various writing assignments, as well as offer alternate language to fulfill the CCSS.

In this chapter, we have proposed how genre pedagogy might be used as a scaffold for teaching the writing standards in the CCSS. Our analysis of student samples using two frameworks shows the compatibility between the SFL approach and the CCSS. The SFL-based pedagogy offers explicit language that can be applied to the CCSS framework without conflicts. The freedom that is available due to the lack of prescribed pedagogy in the CCSS allows educators to adapt their teaching to include more descriptive language that will enable students a greater understanding of writing.

References

Brown, D. F., & Knowles, T. (2007). *What every middle school teacher should know*. Portsmouth, NH: Heinemann.

Christie, F., & Derewianka, B. (2008). *School discourse: Learning to write across the years of schooling*. New York: Continuum.

de Oliveira, L. (2011). A linguistic approach in culturally and linguistically diverse classrooms: A focus on teacher education. *Linguistics and the Human Sciences, 4*(2), 101–159. http://dx.doi.org/10.1558/lhs.v4i2.101

Martin, J. R., & Rose, D. (2008) *Genre relations: Mapping culture*. London: Equinox.

National Governors Association Center for Best Practices & Council of Chief State School Officers (NGA & CCSSO). (2010a). *Common core state standards for English language arts & literacy in history/social studies, science & technical subjects*. Retrieved from http://www.corestandards.org/the-standards

National Governors Association Center for Best Practices & Council of Chief State School Officers (NGA & CCSSO). (2010b). *Common core state standards: Appendix C*. Retrieved from http://www.corestandards.org/the-standards

National Governors Association Center for Best Practices & Council of Chief State School Officers (NGA & CCSSO). (2010c). *Common core state standards: Appendix A*. Retrieved from http://www.corestandards.org/the-standards

Rose, D., & Martin, J. R. (2012). *Learning to write, reading to learn: Genre, knowledge and pedagogy in the Sydney School*. Sheffield: Equinox.

Schleppegrell, M. J. (2004). *The language of schooling: A functional linguistics perspective*. Mahwah, NJ: Erlbaum.

Schleppegrell, M. J., & de Oliveira, L. C. (2006). An integrated language and content approach for history teachers. *Journal of English for Academic Purposes, 5*(4), 254–268. http://dx.doi.org/10.1016/j.jeap.2006.08.003

9 Standardized assessments for English language learners: implications of differing expectations

Deedra A. Arvin and Dominique Lowery Franklin

In this chapter, informational passages used in high-stakes testing in Indiana for high school students are analyzed and compared. An informational text from the Sample Items posted for the Language Assessment System Links Assessment (LAS Links), which is used in Indiana to determine English language proficiency of English language learners (ELLs), was analyzed. In addition, an informational reading passage from the Item Sampler for the Indiana Statewide Testing for Educational Progress-Plus (ISTEP+) English 10 End of Course Assessment (ECA) was selected. This particular passage is one of three examples provided in the Item Sampler posted on the Indiana Department of Education's website. Because an informational passage for LAS Links grades 9–12 was analyzed, the informational passage from the ISTEP+ English 10 ECA Item Sampler was selected for comparison. The chapter's analytical focus will be on the textual metafunction. In particular, both thematic development and cohesion are analyzed for both texts, and potential challenges for ELLs are identified. Differences between the sample passages for the two assessments are described, and implications of these differences are discussed.

The LAS Links Assessments, created by CTB/McGraw-Hill, are criterion-referenced assessments used to determine a student's level of English proficiency and to determine which ELL services are appropriate for each student. The Elementary and Secondary Education Act mandates that all students with limited English proficiency will be administered an English language proficiency test each year (ESEA, Section 1111 (b) (7)). Any newly enrolled student who has indicated a language other than English on his or her Home Language Survey is administered an English language proficiency test. In Indiana, the English language proficiency test is the LAS Links Placement

Test (IDOE, n.d.). The LAS Links Annual Assessment is administered each spring to students who are classified as Levels 1–4 on the LAS Links Placement Tests or who have not achieved FEP (fluent English proficient; Level 5) for two consecutive years on the summative assessment (IDOE, n.d.). During a student's first year of U.S. schooling, the LAS Links Annual Assessment may be substituted for the English/Language Arts portion of the ISTEP+ assessment (IDOE, 2012). Students who score at Levels 1–4 are eligible for accommodations, such as small-group administration, spelling aid, extended time, and text read aloud on the English/Language Arts portion of the ISTEP+. Not only is the annual assessment used to determine the student's current level of English proficiency, it also serves as an accountability measure for school districts. LAS Links results are used to determine district- and school-level Annual Measurable Achievement Objectives.

The LAS Links Assessment measures speaking, listening, reading, and writing, and provides a measure of comprehension skills in academic and social English language. It is administered to students in five grade bands: K–1, 2–3, 4–5, 6–8, and 9–12. The test format includes content-area (mathematics, science and technology, reading/language arts, and social studies) multiple-choice and performance-based questions to address the various language skills within the four domains: Listening, Speaking, Reading, and Writing.

The ISTEP+ ECA for English 10 is one of three course-specific, criterion-referenced assessments designed to assess the student's mastery of the Indiana Academic Standards. The other two course-specific ECAs are Algebra I and Biology I. Students in Indiana are required to pass the Algebra I and English 10 assessments in order to meet the graduation testing requirement of the state. The ECA English 10 assessment measures Reading Comprehension and Writing Applications and is administered to high school students during completion of English 10, which is typically offered in the tenth grade.

Textual analysis of LAS links

Our analysis focuses on the Reading Comprehension portion of the test for students in grades 9–12. For the reading comprehension section, students are instructed to read a passage and answer associated questions. The questions address three sub-skills: demonstrating reading comprehension, identifying important literary features of text, and applying learning strategies to interpretation. We have selected an informational reading passage from the Sample Test Items of the LAS Links K–12 Assessments. Indiana, like most other states in the United States, has adopted the Common Core State Standards for English Language Arts, which places an increased emphasis on informational texts, especially in the high school grades where it is recommended that 70% of the texts that students read are informational (Calkins, Ehrenworth, & Lehman, 2012). This emphasis on informational texts comes from the 2009 reading framework of the National Assessment of Educational Progress (NAEP) in an effort to increase the number of students who can meet the requirements needed to be considered college and career ready (National Governors Association Center for Best Practices & Council of Chief State School Officers, 2010). Many students in secondary grades are unable to access the complex and often dense texts of secondary subjects that allow them to succeed in college and careers, and ELLs are heavily and disproportionately represented among these struggling readers (Fang & Schleppegrell, 2008). Therefore, it is important to understand the difficulties that informational texts pose for ELLs and whether the difficulties posed by the texts in LAS Links are representative of those which students will encounter in academic texts.

This text analysis provides a baseline for what is expected to assess the English proficiency levels of all Indiana high school ELLs in reading as measured by the LAS Links. We have identified features of this text that may cause difficulties in reading comprehension for ELLs. In the following analysis, we focus on the textual metafunction of the text. Textual choices are key to the cohesion and coherence of a text and vary across different modes (Eggins, 1994). According to Christie and Derewianka (2008), "the textual function of language is perhaps the most critical for learners to master as they move from the dynamic and spontaneous oral mode into the more reflective, crafted written texts of schooling" (p. 19). Iddings and de Oliveira (2011) state that the "textual metafunction is responsible for realizing the mode of texts"; therefore, an analysis of Theme, Rheme, and cohesion can help teachers and students understand how the text realizes this level of meaning (p. 36). This is especially important in informational texts, as they differ more significantly from spoken language than narrative texts, making them more difficult for students, especially ELLs, to understand. In this analysis, the Theme is defined as the beginning of the clause and signals the point of departure, while the Rheme provides the new information (Christie & Derewianka, 2008; Martin & Rose, 2008). We use Halliday's (1994) definition of a marked Theme as any Theme that is something other than the Subject. For clarity in the analysis, the numbers added in front of each independent clause are used to indicate the clause number to which we refer in the analysis. The // separates the Theme and Rheme, and marked Themes are indicated by boldface font.

Textual metafunction analysis

Text 1: Sequential Explanation

PHENOMENON
(1) Have you // wondered what happens to newspapers when people finish reading them? (2) **Although some are thrown away**, others // are recycled.

EXPLANATION
(3) Newsprint // is the paper on which newspapers are printed. (4) **Before recycling begins**, household members // place newsprint in piles and bins. (5) It // is best if household members separate old newspapers from other materials like plastic and cardboard to keep the newsprint clean. (6) This // is important because dirty newspapers deteriorate and cannot be recycled into newsprint.

(7) **At the recycling centers**, the newsprint // is first squeezed into blocks and then taken to a paper mill. (8) There, the old newspapers // are placed in a machine that removes staples, glue, metal clips, and other objects.

(9) Ink // is then removed from the newsprint during "de-inking." (10) **During this process**, the paper // is mixed with detergent and air to create bubbles, which absorb the ink from the newsprint. (11) The bubbles, and the ink, // are later washed away with water.

(12) **After this is done**, the clean newsprint // is shredded into small pieces. (13) Shredding the paper // breaks down the fibers of the old newsprint into shorter fibers. (14) The shorter fibers // are then used to create new paper.

EXTENSION (Phase 1)
(15) One problem with recycling newsprint // is lignin, a sticky substance in wood that is mixed with cellulose fibers when the paper is first created. (16) Lignin // is generally removed from high-quality paper, (17) **but** it // is left in newsprint because newspapers are not intended to be kept very long. (18) **Over time, however**, lignin // turns newspapers yellow and brittle. (19) Lignin also // causes newsprint to deteriorate. (20) This, **in turn**, // makes newspapers that are very old unsuitable to be recycled into newsprint, although they can still be recycled into other useful products such as cardboard, kitty litter, garden mulch, and housing insulation.

(Phase 2)
(21) **In addition to making old and low quality paper useful**, recycling newsprint // can save energy, landfill space, and trees. (22) **According to some estimates, for example**, one 30-foot-tall tree // is needed to produce 100 pounds of newsprint, the amount consumed by an average American each year. (23) **By comparison**, more than 500,000 trees // are needed each week to produce all of the Sunday newspapers in the United States. (24) How many trees // can recycling newsprint save? (25) **According to some experts**, every ton of recycled newspaper substituted for non-recycled paper // can save up to 17 trees.

This text was identified as a Sequential Explanation. The Sequential Explanation is one of the four types of explanation genres that explain how processes happen (Martin & Rose, 2008). According to Martin and Rose (2008), "the typical structure of explanations is to start by specifying the Phenomenon to be explained, followed by the implication sequence that explains it, the Explanation stage," and an optional Extension stage (p. 150). Martin and Rose (2008) state that "Sequential Explanations are typically constructed as a series of events, in which an obligatory causal relation is implied between each event" (p. 150). Christie and Derewianka (2008) suggest that a Sequential Explanation "explains some phenomenon by establishing the sequence or order in which things occur, involving several phases" (p. 186). Following the Explanation is an optional Extension phase that provides additional information about the explained Phenomenon. This information can be found either at the beginning or conclusion of an Explanation (Martin & Rose, 2008).

This sample text explains how newspapers are recycled. The Phenomenon to be explained, how newspapers are recycled, is stated in the first two clauses. Clause 1 uses a question, *have you wondered what happens to newspapers when people finish reading them*, to engage the reader with the text while identifying the topic as what may happen to newspapers after people are finished reading them. The Theme is unmarked, *have you*, as this is the most typical way that an interrogative phrase is worded. The writer then transitions to declarative clauses for the majority of the rest of the text, beginning with the identification of the Phenomenon to be explained as the recycling of newspapers through the use of a marked Theme to add emphasis to this topic.

The style of catching the attention of the reader of a text with a question is used frequently in introductions to provide interest and focus (Barnet & Stubbs, 1977). Thus, the use of such a method is important to understand when assessing ELLs' abilities to comprehend texts in English.

Following the Phenomenon is the Explanation stage. This stage provides details about each of the steps used when newspapers are recycled. The text uses an implication sequence that shows a series of two phases succeeding each other. The first phase explains what must be done before recycling begins, and the second phase explains what is done at the recycling center. According to Martin and Rose (2008), it is not necessary to use causal conjunctions such as *because*, *so*, and *therefore* in written explanations because "the [Explanation] genre is typically announced in the Phenomenon stage, so the reader can infer causal relations where they are not stated" (p. 150); however, there are instances where causality is explicit in the sample text. Phase 1 is comprised of clauses 3–6. Explicit causality is found in clause 6 with the use of the word *because*. Implicit causality is found in clauses 4 and 5 with the use of the temporal conjunction *before* and the conditional conjunction *if*. In phase 2, clauses 7–14, there are no words that indicate causality explicitly, and the temporal conjunctions *then* (in clauses 7, 9, and 14) and *after* in clause 12 imply causality. The use of temporal conjunctions to imply causality conflate time and cause. This use of implicit causality in a text can be difficult for ELLs, as readers must establish connections between events and construct logical relationships that may not be highlighted in the text (Achugar & Schleppegrell, 2005).

According to Martin and Rose (2008), "sequential explanations vary widely according to the particular phenomenon being explained" (p. 152). In this text, following the Explanation of the process of recycling newspaper is an optional Extension stage that explains the challenges and benefits of recycling. This stage consists of two phases. The first phase (clauses 15–20) explains a challenge associated with recycling, while the second phase (clauses 21–25) explains the benefits of recycling.

The cohesive devices used in this text may be complex for ELLs. According to Christie and Derewianka (2008), generally, the Theme of a clause serves to "cue to the reader: 'This is what I'm talking about'" (p. 20). Marked Themes are those that are unusual or atypical; in declarative clauses, an unmarked Theme is the subject of the clause, while marked Themes such as independent clauses and prepositional phrases signal that something in the context requires that an atypical meaning will be realized from the text (Eggins, 1994). Marked Themes are present throughout the text in clauses 2, 4, 7, 8, 10, 12, 17, 18, 19, 20, 21, 22, 23, and 25. Students who have difficulty understanding marked Themes will therefore have difficulty comprehending the text. The first marked Theme is presented early in the text in clause 2. *Although some are thrown away* is a prepositional phrase that refers back to a portion of the newspapers that people are done reading (referred to in clause 1) and sets up the remaining papers as the topic of the text. This clause is central in understanding the meaning of the text, as it presents the topic, and the inclusion of pronouns that separate the newspapers referred to in the first clause into two groups may pose a difficulty for ELLs (de Oliveira, 2011). Many of the marked themes (in clauses 4, 7, 8, 10, 12, 18, and 20) are temporal phrases used to improve understanding by identifying the order in which events in the process of recycling occur. *Also*, in clause 19, is a conjunction used to show an additional property of lignin. In clause 21, the phrase *in addition* reminds the reader of information introduced previously before providing a new benefit of recycling newsprint. Clauses 22 and 23 use marked Themes (*according to some estimates*, *for example*, and *by comparison*) that lend authority to the information to follow. Marked Themes are selected by the author when the typical point of departure for a sentence will not adequately convey the meaning of the text that is desired (Eggins, 1994). The types of marked Themes found within this text are commonly found in academic texts, and thus are important to include in an assessment to determine if students have acquired sufficient proficiency in English to be considered able to perform as well as their native English-speaking peers academically.

The writer of the text has used additional cohesive devices to create links within the text (Christie & Derewianka, 2008). The demonstrative found in the Theme of clause 6, *this*, refers back to clause 5, which describes how household members separate old newspapers from other materials to keep the newsprint clean. In clause 10, *this process* refers back to the process of *de-inking* described in clause 9. *It* in clause 17 refers back to *lignin*, which is referred to in clauses 15 and 16. The demonstrative *this* is used again in clause 20, however this time to refer to *lignin* causing newspapers to deteriorate and explaining why newspapers that are very old are unsuitable to be recycled into newsprint. Also in clause 20 is the personal pronoun *they* which refers back to very old newspapers. Several times (e.g., in clauses 5, 7, 8, 10, 12, 13, and 14) the determiner *the* is used to refer back to newsprint, papers, clean newsprint, or fibers that have been previously introduced. While the use of pronouns in the Theme position can aid writers in building a cohesive text, de Oliveira (2011) found that this strategy can hinder comprehension by ELLs due to confusion about what the pronouns are referring to.

Textual analysis of ISTEP+ English 10 ECA

This analysis focuses on the English 10 ECA Reading Comprehension portion of the test, where students are assessed on the following standards:

- Standard 1: Word Recognition, Fluency, and Vocabulary Development;
- Standard 2: Reading Comprehension and Analysis of Nonfiction and Informational Text;
- Standard 3: Reading Comprehension and Analysis of Literary Text (Indiana ECA Test Blueprints, n.d.).

According to the Indiana ECA Test Blueprints, for Standard 1, questions may include determining the meaning of new words in context and identifying the literal and figurative meanings of words. For Standard 2, questions may include analyzing the format and structure of informational texts, evaluating an author's argument, and drawing conclusions about a text using supporting evidence. For Standard 3, questions may include evaluating characters' traits and actions, analyzing plot, identifying literary devices, and explaining how point of view and author's voice affect the meaning of the text.

The sample text for this analysis was identified as an example of the Exposition genre. According to Martin and Rose (2008), the Exposition is the best known of the argumentation genres. In an Exposition, a thesis is described and argued for. The stages of an Exposition are labeled as (Background) ^ Thesis ^ Arguments ^ Reinforcement of Thesis (Christie & Derewianka, 2008).

Text 2: exposition

Watch Your Electronic Footprint

BACKGROUND (optional)

(1) **Scanning the want ads in your local newspaper**, you // find what you think is the perfect summer job. (2) You // submit an application and schedule an interview. (3) **Dressed to impress**, you // meet with your prospective employer, who seems quite taken by your appearance, poise, and eagerness to work. (4) The job // is yours, right?

(5) **Maybe not**, (6) **if** the employer // tracks your electronic footprint.

Life in the Digital Age

(7) Computers, networks, and the worldwide web // have changed the way we share information. (8) Letters and long-distance phone calls // have become passé. (9) **They'//ve** been replaced by text messaging and the Internet phenomenon known as social networking—a quick way to maintain contact with friends and family in a communal on-line space. (10) Most social networking sites // enable users to create their own web pages that include photos, background information, and blogs.

THESIS

(11) **What** network users don't consider, however, // is that these web pages also provide employers with a new, completely legal way to check out potential employees.

ARGUMENT 1

(12) How // so? (13) **Well**, employers // simply have to go to the networking website's home page, join the network, and search for the person they're interested in learning about. (14) **If that person has a web page on that network and if the page has a global access setting**, any and all information posted there // is available for public viewing.

ARGUMENT 2

(15) **If the person's web page has a restricted access setting**, the employer // can ask to join that person's select network of friends. (16) **Of course**, the person // can deny the request, (17) but research // has shown that he or she probably won't. (18) A recent study of 14 to 21 year-olds who use social networks // showed that 66% of them allowed strangers to access their web page.

ARGUMENT 3

(19) Job applicants // should be mindful that personal information might be accessed not only through their own web page but also through those of their friends. (20) The information on friends' pages // may not be accurate. (21) **In addition**, photos on the web // can easily be downloaded, manipulated, and reposted on their web pages. (22) Many social networking sites // allow users to tag photos with names, making it easy for employers to locate images by typing a name into an Internet search engine.

REINFORCEMENT OF THESIS

Does It Matter?

(23) **Perhaps** the willingness of young social networking users to allow free access to their web pages // has something to do with an overall lack of concern about the consequences. (24) The study previously mentioned also // showed that 75% of users were not too worried about "important people" viewing their personal information. (25) **Yet** they // might do well to reconsider that attitude.

(26) Human resource departments increasingly // rely on the Internet to recruit and research workers. (27) One in five employers // uses the Internet to research information on job candidates. (28) Nearly 60% // say that what they find has some bearing on their hiring decisions. (29) **As one company spokesman says**, "Potential employers // are never more than a few clicks away from information about you." (30) **So** // mind // that electronic footprint!

The first stage in an Exposition is the optional Background. The Background provides contextual information about the topic argued (Christie & Derewianka, 2008). In the ISTEP+ ECA sample passage, the context provides information about the process for obtaining a job and how technology has changed the way employers find information about potential candidates. This Background is found in clauses 1–10. This stage contains some marked Themes, including two that describe *you*, the reader who should be watching his or her electronic footprint during the process of looking for the perfect summer job (i.e., *scanning the want ads in your local newspaper*, and *dressed to impress*).

Following the Background stage is the Thesis which "states the general proposition to be argued" (Christie & Derewianka, 2008, p. 133). The Thesis for the passage (clause 11) indicates the position that employers can legally find out a candidate's information that is posted on social websites. In clause 11, ***What** network users don't consider, however, // is that these web pages also provide employers with a new, completely legal way to check out potential employees*, the marked Theme, *What*, could be challenging for ELLs and other struggling readers because the word *What* most commonly signals an interrogative rather than declarative clause. Interpreting the clause in the interrogative mood would change the meaning of the text, as it would question the reader and create confusion for ELLs.

Following the Thesis are the arguments which support the Thesis. Generally, Expositions contain three arguments (Martin & Rose, 2008). The selected text is typical of Expositions in this regard. Argument 1 is comprised of clauses 12–14; Argument 2 is comprised of clauses 15–18; and Argument 3 is comprised of clauses 19–22. The first argument begins with a question, indicating to the reader that a shift is taking place in the text, from one phase to another: "(12) How // so?" The first argument ends with clause 14, which contains the conditional conjunction, *if*: "(14) **If that person has a web page on that network and if the page has a global access setting**, any and all information posted there // is available for public viewing."

Clause 15 shifts to the second argument as indicated again by the conditional conjunction, *if*: "(15) **If the person's web page has a restricted access setting**, the employer // can ask to join that person's select network of friends." This provides an alternate way that employers can research potential employees. The third argument begins with clause 19; the most significant signal to students that the second argument is over and the third is beginning is the change to a new paragraph: "(19) Job applicants // should be mindful that personal information might be accessed not only through their own web page but also through those of their friends."

Each argument describes how employers can legally access information on social websites about potential employees for a given situation. Conditional conjunctions are used to separate the different arguments. Martin and Rose (2008) indicate that "condition modalises a causal event with probability" (p. 150). For example, in the first two arguments, "If that person has a web page on that network and if the page has a global access setting, any and all information posted there is available for public viewing," and "If the person's web page has a restricted access setting, the employer can ask to join that person's select network of friends," the conjunctions expected are *if* and *then*. However, the *then* is implied rather than explicitly appearing in the sentence. *If* is a subordinating conjunction, which is one example of a logical connector. According to Menyuk and Brisk (2005), logical connectors are an example of a language structure that causes problems for ELLs in academic language. In the third argument, "Job applicants should be mindful that personal information might be accessed not only through their own web page but also through those of their friends," the modal verbs *should* and *might* indicate obligation and uncertainty (Fang & Schleppegrell, 2008). For some learners of English, these verbs can be problematic and difficult to understand because their native languages do not have separate categories of verbs (Xu & Bull, 2010). Problems also arise when modality is not explicitly explained to students. Freeman and Freeman (2004) state that although modal verbs may occur in conversational language, they are more common in academic language, suggesting that "students need scaffolded instruction to help understand this complex language" (p. 247).

The final stage of the Exposition is the Reinforcement of Thesis. According to Christie and Derewianka (2008), this stage "reasserts the Thesis in the light of the arguments that have been provided" (p. 134). Clauses 23–30 make up this stage, which reasserts the Thesis and provides additional support for the Thesis. In the Reinforcement, the author uses statistical data as an engagement resource to bring in other perspectives. This engagement resource detaches the author from the issue by attributing the authority to others, providing credibility to the assertions made (Christie & Derewianka, 2008). Not only does this new stage begin with a new paragraph, there is also another text feature that signals a new stage for the reader: a heading, titled *Does It Matter?* which indicates to the reader that information is going to be presented that describes why information in the previous arguments is important.

Several cohesive devices were used in this text to create links. In clause 4, the determiner *the* refers back to *what you think is the perfect summer job*. It was introduced in clause 1 as new information, but now can be taken for granted (Christie & Derewianka, 2008). This determiner is also used to refer back to previous objects in clauses 5, 15, 16, 20, and 24. In clause 5, *maybe not* answers the question posed by question 4. Later in the text, clause 12 uses the same pattern of asking and answering a question to tie the text together and move the explanation along. Clause 9 uses the personal pronoun *they* to refer back to letters and long-distance phone calls described in clause 8. The demonstrative pronoun *these* is used in clause 11 to describe web pages that were described in clause 10. In clause 21, *in addition* adds to the description of how personal information can be accessed on their friends' web pages.

Comparison between the texts

Both texts made use of marked Themes in over half of the clauses. The majority of the marked Themes in the LAS Links passage were dependent clauses indicating when (e.g., *before recycling begins*, *during this process*, or *after this is done*) or where (e.g., *at the recycling centers* or *there*) a part of the recycling process occurs. Other clauses indicate comparison (e.g., *although some are thrown away* and *by comparison*). In the last paragraph, there are two marked Themes that indicate the source of the information that follows (i.e., *according to some estimates* and *according to some experts*). The marked Themes in the ECA passage serve more varied purposes, from conditional phrases that modalize probability (e.g., *if that person has a web page on that network and if the page has a global access setting*, or *if the person's web page has a restricted access setting*) and indicating the source of information (e.g., *as one company spokesman says*) to adverbs that modify the processes later in the sentence (e.g., *perhaps*) and phrases that describe the Theme (e.g., *scanning the want ads in your local newspaper* or *dressed to impress*).

Both texts also made use of a variety of cohesive devices to tie the text together. These included personal pronouns, determiners, comparatives, and demonstratives, as well as other devices, such as phrases in the LAS Links text that indicate the steps in the process of recycling newspaper and asking and answering questions to move forward the argument (that users of social networking should mind their electronic footprint). Cohesion is an important element in texts designed to assess reading comprehension, as it is a key factor in comprehension, especially of non-narrative texts (Christie & Derewianka, 2008).

Some of the features of the two texts exhibited differences that were important. One of those differences was the use of headings, found in the ECA passage, but not in the LAS Links passages. Headings are used to guide a reader of an informational text, thus are a feature of writing that are important for ELLs to be familiar with. Perhaps the lack of headings in the LAS Links passage can be explained by the text being shorter than that used for the ECA; there are 25 clauses in the LAS Links passage and 30 in the ECA passage, which is approximately a paragraph longer. However, this lack of headings can increase the difficulty of comprehending the passage, especially for struggling readers.

Additionally, there were differences in the difficulty of the Processes used in the two texts. In the LAS Links text, the Processes are primarily material, describing "doings and happenings in the material world—'outer' experience" or relational, describing "processes of 'being' and 'having' creating relationships between elements of experience" (Christie & Derewianka, 2008, p. 9), although the text does begin with the mental Process "wondered." The Processes used in the ECA text were more varied and included tenses that are traditionally learned later in school and may be more difficult for ELLs to understand. Unlike the LAS Links passage, the ECA passage includes few material Processes (e.g., submit or meet). Verbal Processes (e.g., say, deny, or ask), mental Processes (e.g., consider or reconsider), and relational Processes (e.g., have become, is available, or has shown) can be found throughout the ECA passage. The variety and difficulty of these Processes as compared to those in the LAS Links passage indicate that this text is likely more difficult for ELLs and other struggling readers to comprehend.

We found many similarities and differences when comparing these two texts. Although some features used are similar across the texts, overall these features (and others) were applied in such a way that the sample text from the ECA is more difficult for ELLs than the sample text from the LAS Links assessment. The difficulty of an assessment is often thought to be dependent upon the questions that are asked of the students about the texts they read. However, ACT found in their 2006 study that, while the difficulty and type of questions did not differentiate between students who met the benchmark of readiness for college and students who did not, students who were successful in understanding more complex texts were more likely to be considered ready for college. Therefore, although there are a few sample questions available for each of the sample passages, we did not include them in our analysis. Additionally, we realize that a range of passages are used on each assessment, with some texts being more complex or having features more difficult for ELLs than others.

Implications for teachers

Through this analysis, we found that the English language skills required on the English 10 ECA were more rigorous than those required on the state's English language proficiency assessment. The differences relate to the complexity of the texts that students are expected to read and understand rather than differences in the types of questions asked of students on the different assessments. Special attention should be given to marked Themes found in informational texts, as they are common, especially in the academic texts that students will need to be successful in college and careers.

Teachers in Indiana should be aware that students who score at high levels on the LAS Links assessment may not truly possess the level of reading comprehension in English required to be successful on the English 10 ECA. Teachers in other states may find the same results when comparing texts used on their states' English language proficiency assessments with those on their high school English language arts assessments. Although students may be classified as FEP and exit ELL programs, ELL students may still struggle with complex texts, especially informational texts. Teachers should also be aware that ELLs will continue to need instructional support even if state laws do not mandate such efforts.

This analysis should serve as a caveat for teachers that students need access to rich complex informational texts in the classroom, or they will not be prepared for the English 10 ECA.

Based on our analysis, it appears that both texts meet their purpose of assessing reading comprehension of academic English; however, the level of complexity creates a differing standard for which ELLs must achieve. As

ELLs reach a level 5 score on LAS Links, they are considered fluent English proficient and no longer receive ELL services in school. They no longer receive testing accommodations or classroom instructional modifications, but are expected to achieve the same academic standard as their English-speaking peers. Interestingly, although a student's LAS Links scores may consider the student to be FEP, the complexity of the LAS Links text does not equate to the complexity of the text found on the English 10 ECA. As the ECA standards transition to Common Core State Standards, the expectation is that the rigor and complexity of text will increase, thus causing a greater demand for the explicit teaching of complex texts to all learners, with special attention to the language needs of ELLs.

References

Achugar, M., & Schleppegrell, M. J. (2005). Beyond connectors: The construction of cause in history textbooks. *Linguistics and Education, 16*, 298–318. http://dx.doi.org/10.1016/j.linged.2006.02.003

ACT. (2006). *Reading between the lines: What the ACT reveals about college readiness in reading.* Iowa City: Author. Retrieved from www.act.org/research /policymakers/pdf/ reading_report.pdf

Barnet, S., & Stubbs, M. (1977). *Barnet & Stubb's practical guide to writing* (Rev. ed.). Boston: Little, Brown and Company.

Calkins, L., Ehrenworth, M., & Lehman, C. (2012). *Pathways to the common core: Accelerating achievement*. Portsmouth, NH: Heinemann.

Christie, F., & Derewianka, B. (2008). *School discourse: Learning to write across the years of schooling.* New York: Continuum.

de Oliveira, L. C. (2011). *Knowing and writing school history: The language of students' expository writing and teachers' expectations.* Charlotte, NC: Information Age Publishing.

Eggins, S. (1994). *An introduction to systemic functional linguistics*. London: Pinter Publishers.

Fang, Z., & Schleppegrell, M. J. (2008). *Reading in secondary content areas: A language-based pedagogy.* Ann Arbor, MI: University of Michigan Press.

Freeman, D. E., & Freeman, Y. S. (2004). *Essential linguistics: What you need to know to teach reading, ESL, spelling, phonics, and grammar.* Portsmouth, NH: Heinemann.

Halliday, M. A. K. (1994). *An introduction to functional grammar* (2nd ed.). London: Edward Arnold.

Iddings, J., & de Oliveira, L.C. (2011). Applying the genre analysis of a narrative to the teaching of English language learners. *INTESOL Journal, 8*(1), 25–41.

IDOE Office of Student Assessment. (2012). *2011–2012 ISTEP+ program manual: Policies and procedures for Indiana's assessment system.* Retrieved from: http://www.doe.in.gov/sites/default/files/assessment/2011-12-istep-program-manual2-23-12.pdf

IDOE Office of Student Assessment (n.d.). *LAS Links FAQ*. Retrieved from:

http://www.doe.in.gov/sites/default/files/assessment/las-links-faq2.pdf

Martin, J. R., & Rose, D. (2008). *Genre relations: Mapping culture*. London: Equinox.

Menyuk, P., & Brisk, M. E. (2005). *Language development and education: Children with varying language experience.* New York: Palgrave Macmillan. http://dx.doi.org/10.1057/9780230504325

National Governors Association Center for Best Practices & Council of Chief State School Officers (NGA & CCSSO). (2010). *Common Core State Standards for English language arts and literacy in history/social studies, science, and technical subjects*. Washington, DC: Authors. Retrieved from http://www.corestandards.org /assets/CCSSI_ELA%20Standards.pdf

Xu, J., & Bull, S. (2010). Encouraging advanced second language speakers to recognise their language difficulties: A personalised computer-based approach. *Computer Assisted Language Learning, 23*(2), 111–127. http://dx.doi.org/10.1080/09588221003666206

10 Writing a dissertation proposal: genre expectations

Joshua G. Iddings, Shu-Wen Lan, and Luciana C. de Oliveira

The writing of a dissertation proposal (DP) can be a daunting task. This can be particularly true if the new scholar lacks models when developing their research plans. Knowledge of the essential genre stages and phases of DPs and the aims and purposes of writing DPs is essential. In addition, new scholars need knowledge of the linguistic characteristics of DPs. However, there are very few examples in the literature which cover these aspects of this very important genre in a graduate student's career. This chapter aims to address some of these issues for graduate students using qualitative research methods within the discipline of education. While it is impossible to know exactly what all DPs should encompass—and these issues should always be negotiated with one's academic advisor(s)—we identify here several key genre and linguistic features for understanding the language of DPs in our own field. In this chapter, we accomplish several important tasks related to the composition of DPs in education. We begin by briefly reviewing literature based in the writing of DPs in general. Then, we discuss the relevant elements of systemic functional linguistics (SFL) we used to both analyze a model DP (from our advisor, Luciana) and then compose our own (Josh and Shu-Wen) DPs. Finally, using examples from these three different DPs, we discuss the structure and language of the DP.

Literature review

The relevant research concerning the writing of DPs is relatively limited. Often, books and articles which explore the challenges of writing DPs, and other research projects like them, are concerned with helping researchers learn how to manage their writing process in order to complete the project in a timely manner (Silva, 2007). A number of publications are available to help with this very important part of the research process (Belcher, 2009; Glatthorn, 1998; Krathwohl & Smith, 2005; Meloy, 2001). However, there are very few examples of publications that go beyond either the writing process or the general stages involved in the construction of the DP. Or, as is the case with Meloy (2001), the publication discusses what a dissertation "looks like" (p. 2) without actually discussing the language used to write the dissertation or proposal with any depth. For those publications that discuss the general stages of DPs, most often the focus is on the rhetorical content of each stage, where very little attention is paid to the linguistic challenges and requirements of constructing the DP. It is important to recognize that the task of constructing the DP has its own expected ways of using language. Kilbourn (2006) points out that,

> [t]he proposal is an academic document, and consequently its stock-and-trade is academic prose. Even though what is being proposed might be unusual or unorthodox, the means for proposing it are defensible, reasoned arguments. There is an art of writing a good proposal (and good proposals are carefully crafted), but in the end, a proposal is an academic document, not a literary one, and straightforward clarity about what, why, how, who, and when is critical. (pp. 535–536)

Not all PhD students are equally prepared to face the task of constructing the DP in expected ways (i.e., using academic prose, linguistically constructing defensible, reasoned arguments, and linguistically organizing the DP for that straightforward clarity). Simultaneously, not all PhD students share the same understanding that certain ways of constructing the DP through language are expected by their advisor and committee. By focusing primarily on the language of organization of DPs, this chapter provides detailed descriptions of each of the primary stages and phases in the DP as they connect to the linguistic resources used to organize them.

Methods

For the purpose of our analysis, we have utilized Macken-Horarik (2002) as a way of framing the rhetorical context one must consider when writing a DP. In this framework, Macken-Horarik (2002) identifies and explains four important aspects of a genre analysis: the social purpose, social location, schematic structure, and schematic description of the genre being written. This allows the analyst, and in our case the student researcher, to understand the contextual issues affecting the language used in a DP.

In addition to the rhetorical considerations of the DP, we also analyzed the thematic development of the DP using SFL (Halliday & Matthiessen, 2004; Martin & Rose, 2008). The overall theoretical underpinnings of our analysis were discussed in Chapter 1 of this collection. However, for the sake of making this analysis more approachable for student researchers outside the SFL tradition, we have also altered some of the language that we use to talk about our analysis and the results. For example, instead of discussing the SFL concepts of Theme and hyper-Theme, we have chosen to present these in terms of Signaling the Phase. Signaling phases within genre stages is one of the functions of thematic development and was found to be quite important for the DP genre.

Results

In this section, we present the results and discussion of our analysis. First, we present the social purpose and social location of the DP in general. We then provide the overall schematic structure of the DP (Figure 10.1), including the major stages and phases within each stage. As we present each major stage in succession, we also discuss the overall goals and purposes of each stage along with the goals and purposes of each phase. Finally, we give examples from the DPs of Luciana, Josh, and Shu-Wen to illustrate several key linguistic characteristics that we believe will help student researchers construct their own DPs. In this chapter, we focus on a Theme analysis that we call Signaling the Phase, where we describe the Theme and sometimes the hyper-Theme development of each phase.

Social purpose and location of the dissertation proposal

The DP is a formal academic text which is an important step in qualifying for writing and defending the dissertation. Typically, students work through writing their DP with the aid of an advisor who guides them through the construction of the proposal and helps them understand the necessary components. Once the DP is submitted, the student researcher must defend their research questions and methodology, arguing why the research is a novel contribution to the discipline. Finally, after successfully defending the DP, and making pertinent revisions, the student submits a final DP. This is a high-stakes endeavor. An unsuccessful DP or defense can be a major setback for both the research project itself and for the completion of the graduate degree.

Stages and phases of the dissertation proposal

Writing a DP is a challenging literacy task and takes a series of rhetorical moves to complete, known here as stages and phases. The genre analysis of the DPs for this chapter revealed that each consisted of four primary stages: 1) Rationale, 2) Literature Review, 3) Methods, and 4) Significance and Implications. The following section gives an overall picture of the DP, including the four primary stages in bold and the many phases within each stage in the order in which they appear in the DP.

Figure 10.1. The overall schematic structure of the DP

The Rationale stage

The overall goal of the Rationale stage is to provide information for the research questions a student researcher is exploring and why she/he selected such research questions. We call this a process of building field generally. To allow readers to better understand the rationale for selecting the research questions, the DP writer is expected to contextualize the selected research topic and questions. Giving a description of personal involvement in the research topic can be one way to contextualize the study. For example, using Luciana's DP as a model, Shu-Wen's personal experience contributed to her selection of her specific research topic and the related research questions which Shu-Wen discussed in her Rationale. Including contextualized information and personal connections to the selected research topic and questions within the first primary stage can deepen readers' understanding of the research.

Signaling the phase. In this section, we name each phase within the Rationale stage of the proposal, providing a description of the linguistic characteristics of each phase. We identified five phases as outlined in Table 10.1 below.

Table 10.1. The five phases of the Rationale stage

Phase Number	Title of Phase
1	Orientation
2	Researcher's Perspective
3	Purpose of the Study
4	Generative Promise
5	Outline of the DP

The Orientation phase tends to be a paragraph informing readers how the DP writer became interested in the selected research topic and research questions. An example of signaling the Orientation phase can be seen in Luciana's DP.

Text 10.1

Phase 1	(Luciana's DP example)
Orientation (extract only)	Many middle and secondary history teachers often report the difficulties of teaching writing in history. Also, many teachers feel unprepared to teach writing because they themselves were not taught writing and/or not prepared by their credential programs to teach writing in the subject matter they are teaching. They also feel unprepared to deal with the challenges of helping English language learners (ELLs) and low literacy students. In addition, very little research has been done on student writing in history.

By beginning with the Theme in the first sentence *Many middle and secondary history teachers* (Text 10.1), Luciana introduces the problem encountered by the specific group of teachers—middle and secondary history teachers. This Theme is then followed by Themes in the following sentences, *Also, many teachers* and *They also*, signaling that she further identifies the challenges encountered by these middle and secondary history teachers in teaching writing. Also, *In addition, very little research*, signals that there are very few related studies on teaching history writing to support and guide middle and secondary history teachers. Here, we see how Luciana argues for the worth of the research topic and research questions selected for her research.

The Researcher's Perspective phase functions to provide specific information about why the DP writer has passion for researching the educational phenomenon selected. As seen in Luciana's DP (Text 10.2), due to her previous professional experience, Luciana recognizes the specific challenges encountered by middle and secondary history teachers. Especially noteworthy in this example is her use of first person pronouns (*me*, *my*) to express her personal working experiences with teachers in the history project.

Text 10.2

Phase 2	(Luciana's DP example)
Researcher's Perspective (extract only)	These problems are evident to me in my own work with the California History-Social Science Project (CH-SSP) … As one of the literacy leaders of this program at the History and Cultures Project (HCP) from UC Davis, my main responsibility is assisting in the development of curricula and guiding history teachers in the application of different literacy strategies.

In the Purpose of the Study phase, the DP writer explains the research questions set within the context of the field of study. The purpose of this phase is to inform readers which research questions the writer plans to explore in the study and how the writer will answer these questions. As seen in Text 10.3, Luciana focuses on what she will do about the proposed research questions, including what she will achieve by conducting the study and how she will analyze the collected student essays.

Text 10.3

Phase 3	(Luciana's DP example)
Purpose of the Study (extract only)	The proposed study will address the problems presented above by answering the following research questions...

In the Generative Promise phase, the DP writer focuses on the potential contribution of the proposed dissertation study for a particular audience. As Luciana's DP shows, she first identifies the valuable contribution SFL literacy researchers have made towards diverse students' writing development in Australia. She then points out she would further the contribution of SFL literacy research in the U.S. K–12 context (*I would be able to further this work by ...*) (Text 10.4).

Text 10.4

Phase 4	(Luciana's DP example)
Generative Promise (extract only)	Functional linguistic research in Australia has demonstrated that there are significant differences in terms of the grammatical resources used by students when writing at different points in their schooling (Coffin, 1997; 2004). I would be able to further this work by focusing on students in California in middle (eighth grade) and secondary (eleventh grade) school history by identifying resources needed for school success in history and showing whether and how they differ as students move from middle to high school in U.S. History classes.

In the Outline of the Dissertation Proposal phase, the DP writer describes a likely structure for the final product that will be written, providing readers with a map of the structure of the subsequent sections of dissertation proposal. In the example from Luciana's DP (Text 10.5), we can see she accomplishes this by showing how she will structure the various sections of the DP (*This proposal will begin with ..., Following the review of these literatures ..., Subsequently, data collection and analytical methodologies will be outlined* ...).

Text 10.5

Phase 5	(Luciana's DP example)
Outline of the DP (extract only)	This proposal will begin with a review of the literature pertaining to various aspects of historical understanding and school history writing. Following the review of these literatures, I will suggest that there are gaps in the knowledge base as it pertains to school history writing and the role language plays in students' demonstration of their historical understanding. Subsequently, data collection and analytical methodologies will be outlined followed by a discussion of the significance of the proposed research. I finalize the proposal with some potential implications for educational practice.

The Literature Review stage

The Literature Review is the section of the DP where the student expresses their proficiency in knowing the relevant literature in the academic area in which they will be completing their dissertation. It is through the Literature Review that the student shows that they have indeed read the literature and can situate their study within this literature to show they have a study worth undertaking that will contribute to their academic discipline. In general, the student should be careful to organize the Literature Review in a logical way that makes sense for their project. We have found that many novice researchers organize their scholarship according to what we call the "shopping list" manner of organization. That is, the organization is based on listing the individual contributions of other scholars, often represented by paragraph organization centering on the author of a scholarly piece rather than being organized thematically by the content Themes of many different authors' contributions in the discipline. We will take up this issue later when discussing the organization of the Literature Review. While we have stated that the purpose of the Rationale stage is for "building field generally," the overall purpose of the Literature Review is for building field specifically. Here, we mean that the Literature Review is a survey of the scholarship that has been produced specific to the discipline being investigated and builds up the field of knowledge for the discipline, understanding what scholars have specifically been investigating across the field of study.

Signaling the phase. In this section, we name each phase within the Literature Review stage of the proposal, providing a description of the linguistic teristics of each phase. We identified six phases as outlined in Table 10.2 below.

Table 10.2. The six phases of the Literature Review stage

Phase Number	Title of Phase
1	Introduction
2	Outline of Literature Review
3	Thematically Organized Review of Multiple Sources
4	Specific Focus on Several Key Studies
5	Limitations of Other Literature in the Field
6	Overall Summary of the Research in the Field

The Introduction phase tends to be a paragraph describing why the proposed study is of interest in the field in which the student intends to investigate. An example of signaling this stage can be seen in the first two sentences of Luciana's Introduction phase in her Literature Review (Text 10.6). Here, Luciana orients the reader to the important issue which she will take up in her dissertation project. She hints at the gap she found during the process of reviewing the scholarship in her field. By using the Theme, "The ability of students to demonstrate their historical understanding in writing," the reader

Text 10.6

Phase 1	(Luciana's DP example)
Introduction (extract only)	The ability of students to demonstrate their historical understanding in writing is generally recognized as an area of interest and concern (Young & Leinhardt, 1998; Wineburg, 1994, 2001). Little research has addressed …

immediately can recognize what her paragraph, and thus the phase, will be about. This Theme is juxtaposed with the Theme of the next sentence, "Little research," signaling to the reader that there has been a major gap in the literature because there is "little research" in the area in which she aims to investigate. Thus, we see the importance of the thematic development of the introductory paragraph to orient us to the research and scholarly gaps which will be further discussed in the Literature Review stage of Luciana's DP.

The second phase, Outline of Literature Review, is a paragraph which tells the reader how the overall Literature Review will be organized. While this phase is rather straightforward, it should not be taken lightly for it signals to the reader the initial logical sequence through which the student's argument for their own research will unfold. In this example from Josh's DP (Text 10.7), we see that he has signaled to the reader his overall organization of the Literature Review by pointing out he will draw from two bodies of scholarship.

Text 10.7

Phase 2	(Josh's DP example)
Outline of Literature Review	The following sections provide a review of many important studies in the areas of writing instruction and systemic functional linguistics. This literature review is organized as two larger categories because of the nature of my study. The first section will discuss the modern literature concerning the teaching of writing in the U.S. The second section will focus on SFL theory and its uses in education. These two areas of the literature correlate with my dissertation aims, to show how writing is taught in the U.S. and how SFL might be used to enhance writing pedagogy.

This organization fits his DP, because part of his aim is to situate his study within the discipline of writing instruction, but he also aims to use a lesser-known theory of linguistics to discuss ways in which writing pedagogy can be improved. Thus, he tells the reader that he must first discuss how writing is currently taught and then show how a linguistics approach might aid in this instruction.

While the first two phases of the Literature Review do not actually review much literature, the third phase begins the main focus of the Literature Review and aims to build up the author's field of knowledge within the academic discipline. As mentioned above, the goal here is to give an overview of the scholarly literature which will help the student situate her/his own study within the field. This phase should be organized by major themes across the discipline, rather than through a paragraph by paragraph summary of what authors have said in the discipline. To illustrate this point, below we see two paragraph-initial sentences from one of Josh's previous research papers (Text 10.8 and Text 10.9), that if included in this phase, would not have fit the purpose of the phase.

Text 10.8

Phase 3	(Josh's DP example)
Thematically Organized Review of Multiple Sources (extract only)	Gregory (1987) discusses the theoretical framework of the metafunctions and their use within SFL.

Text 10.9

Phase 3	(Josh's DP example)
Thematically Organized Review of Multiple Sources (extract only)	Ventola (1995) argues for a linguistic backbone for the many rhetorical strategies offered by composition instructors.

Considering the Themes of each paragraph, we see that Josh has organized them based on the article he is reviewing, not based on the Themes of a number of scholars. While the next phase of the Literature Review shows the importance of such paragraph organization, in this phase the purpose is to give a more general overview of the scholarship in the field. The above examples would be better placed in Phase 4 if they are indeed pivotal studies in the field. As an example of a better organized Phase 3 paragraph, we have the first sentence of one of Shu-Wen's Phase 3 paragraphs (Text 10.10). The Theme of this paragraph, "The conceptualization of learning science as learning to talk science," is a nominalized concept important to Shu-Wen's own research. As opposed to Josh's examples above, we see that Shu-Wen has not merely provided a "shopping list" of the latest research in her field. She has instead signaled the organization of this paragraph around a larger theme within education, noting multiple scholarly pieces that have taken up this issue in education research.

Text 10.10

Phase 3	(Shu-Wen's DP example)
Thematically Organized Review of Multiple Sources (extract only)	The conceptualization of learning science as learning to talk science has been proposed by Lemke (1983, 1990, 2001), Wells (1999), among others. Learning to talk science is very much in alignment with recent science reform efforts that emphasize communication of scientific ideas in science teaching and learning.

Once the student has given a more complete picture of the research which has been written in her/his field, the next phase of the Literature Review becomes important. In Phase 4, the author focuses on those key studies which are more intimately connected to their own research proposal. The author has done the work of situating their study in their discipline in general, now they must explore those pivotal studies which they may be drawing from or arguing against in their own dissertation. The paragraphs in this phase will help to show how the student's study will improve the body of knowledge or is less limited in some ways than other studies. We have provided two examples of successful Phase 4 Themes from Luciana's proposal below (Text 10.11 and Text 10.12). These examples show that each paragraph is organized by the important concepts from an individual scholar.

Text 10.11

Phase 4	(Luciana's DP example)
Specific Focus on Several Key Studies (extract only)	Organizational patterns, including connectors as well as the use of documents, were also analyzed in Leinhardt's (2000) study.

Text 10.12

Phase 4	(Luciana's DP example)
Specific Focus on Several Key Studies (extract only)	Coffin (2004) investigated the role of causality in secondary school student writing in history, following a functional linguistic framework.

We see two different ways of signaling here. In the first example the author organizes the paragraph through the concept she/he will explore in their own DP. However, Luciana's example uses "Coffin (2004)" as the Theme to signal the centrality of this study to her DP. While there are different ways to signal the paragraphs in this stage, each way is connected to the overall purpose of discussing specific examples of key articles for the author's own DP.

The purpose of the fifth phase in Literature Review is for the author to discuss the limitations of the existing scholarship in the discipline. This serves to begin showing the differences in the student's own research as opposed to the field at large. We have provided two examples of Themes from both Luciana's (Text 10.13) and Josh's proposal (Text 10.14).

Text 10.13

Phase 5	(Luciana's DP example)
Limitations of Other Literature in the Field (extract only)	While the focus on connectors is crucial for understanding student writing (Leinhardt, 2000), other textual resources also have a key role in constructing historical discourse, as shown in functionally oriented research (Coffin, 1997, 2004; Eggins, Wignell, & Martin, 1993; Martin, 2002; Veel & Coffin 1996; Unsworth, 1999).

Text 10.14

Phase 5	(Josh's DP example)
Limitations of Other Literature in the Field (extract only)	In addition to the concerns with language as a socially constructed phenomenon, post-processes advocates have discussed the problems with the lack of recognition of the diversity of our modern school setting (Pare, 2006).

In Luciana's example, we see her setting up the opposition of scholarship through the use of the connector "while." This serves to signal that Luciana will be countering previous understanding of the role of connectors in her study in terms of the "other textual resources" that are also "key in constructing historical discourse." In Josh's example, this phase is signaled by a different kind of functional word. Here, Josh acknowledges the contributions that have been made to his discipline, all while setting up a dichotomy between his work and the work that has been previously done in the field. Josh achieves this through the use of the "in addition" connector to immediately signal that new information will be discussed "in addition" to the knowledge previously covered in prior phases.

In the final phase of the Literature Review stage, the researcher extends the previous knowledge in the field by showing the reader why their own study will be valuable and add to the knowledge-base of the discipline. In the two examples below (Text 10.15 and Text 10.16), each author begins this phase's paragraph by acknowledging prior scholarship but also mentions the limitations of the scholarship to that point. In these examples, we see that each author guides the reader to the final argument as to why their study is needed.

Text 10.15

Phase 6	(Shu-Wen's DP example)
Limitations of Other Literature in the Field (extract only)	The ability of students to communicate scientific ideas in classroom talk has been recognized as an area of interest and concern (Lemke, 1990; Wells, 1999). A review of the literature on learning science from classroom discourse (e.g., Gibbons, 1999; Lemke, 1990) suggests that there is more to learn about students' development of scientific understandings and scientific language, particularly as it relates to intertextual connections that teachers and students make in classroom discourse.

Text 10.16

Phase 6	(Luciana's DP example)
Limitations of Other Literature in the Field (extract only)	In general, research on historical understanding and its display in writing is limited.

One of the main goals of each project is to contribute new knowledge to the field of study. In order to complete the justification of the study, all of the previous phases must be well argued. By completing previous phases successfully, the author then is able to shift attention away from prior knowledge and towards the importance of filling in the research gap with the research that is being proposed. These arguments are put forth successfully partly through the logic that is displayed when the author signals the phase for the reader.

The Methods stage

The next stage of the DP is the Methods stage. The overall purpose of this stage is for the student researcher to explain the ways in which she/he will gather, analyze, and use the data throughout the dissertation project. The student researcher describes how they will choose their participants, what analytical tools they will use, how they will handle issues of validity and reliability of their results, and how each of the different data they collect will contribute to the overall picture they are trying to paint with their dissertation project. Finally, the student should show why their choice of method(s) will ultimately answer their research questions and why the methods they choose are the best for doing so.

Signaling the phase. In this section, we name each phase within the Methods stage of the proposal, providing a description of the linguistic characteristics of each phase. We identified seven phases as outlined in Table 10.3 below.

Table 10.3. The seven phases of the Methods stage

Phase Number	Title of Phase
1	Context for the Study
2	Roles of the Researcher
3	Data Collection Procedures
4	Participants
5	Data Analysis
6	Data Analysis Table
7	Timelines

In this phase of the Methods, Context for the Study, the writer gives more detailed information about the background of the study. Writers can achieve this in a number of ways. In Text 10.17, Luciana has begun this phase by talking about the challenges that she has set up from previous sections of the DP. She does this by using the "challenges" of teaching "students from diverse backgrounds" as her key points of departure for the background of the study. In Text 10.18, Shu-Wen uses a slightly different approach by utilizing her "research questions" as a thematic transition from her previous DP sections. Regardless, here each writer uses these Themes as transition into the rest of their Methods stage.

Text 10.17

Phase 1	(Luciana's DP example)
Context for the Study (extract only)	Facing challenges in teaching students from diverse backgrounds and developing standards-based curriculum, history teachers have reported the need to strengthen their strategies and increase student achievement in history.

Text 10.18

Phase 1	(Shu-Wen's DP example)
Context for the Study (extract only)	In order to answer the research questions, I choose to work within discourse analysis in application of systemic functional linguistics (SFL), intertextual analysis, and a case study method.

In the next phase, Roles of the Researcher, the DP writer discusses her/his own role(s) in the research atmosphere they are exploring for the dissertation. This section covers many aspects for the study. The research should discuss their duties in the study, whether they will have an intervention, whether they are an insider or outsider to the participants and the community.

Text 10.19

Phase 2	(Josh's DP example)
Roles of the Researcher (extract only)	As the researcher I have to be very careful with my role and the way I manage my identity and my presence in the school.

In Text 10.19, Josh signals the beginning of this phase by using the phrase *As the researcher I* ..., where he inserts himself personally into the research, all the while acknowledging his role as the researcher.

Text 10.20

Phase 2	(Luciana's DP example)
Roles of the Researcher (extract only)	My main duties include development of curricula that integrate literacy strategies in history for the summer literacy institute and year-round guidance in the application of different literacy strategies by history teacher-leaders working with the history project.

In Text 10.20, Luciana takes a similar approach by using *my main duties* as her Theme in the first sentence of this phase. Both writers utilize personal pronouns in the Themes of this phase because the purpose of the section is to discuss their personal role in the research project.

The purpose of the third phase, Data Collection Procedures, is for the writer to discuss what data they will collect and why these data will be pertinent to their research questions. In addition, because the researcher might be answering multiple research questions, the author must tell the reader which questions the data will answer. The Themes here tend to be less personal than other sections.

Text 10.21

Phase 3	(Shu-Wen's DP example)
Data Collection Method (extract only)	Data for this proposed study will be collected by means of classroom observations and interviews with the teacher.

In Text 10.21, Shu-Wen uses the Theme *data for this proposed study* to signal the beginning of this section. As such, the rest of the phase moves on to discuss the various ways in which data will be collected. Here, Shu-Wen does not use any personal pronouns within her Theme, suggesting neutrality in the data collection procedures.

The purpose of the next phase, Participants, is for the writer to introduce the reader to the participants from whom data will be collected. This phase is a natural progression from the previous one, as it involves a more detailed account of the people involved in the qualitative project and an argument as to why these participants will be participating. The writer must justify why each participant is central to the study and how the data collected will contribute to answering the central research questions. As the hyper-Theme of the section, Luciana's example in Text 10.22 shows the transition to this new phase of the DP.

Text 10.22

Phase 4	(Luciana's DP example)
Participants (extract only)	I will interview the California History-Social Science Project's two main directors, the executive director and the associate director, who are the most familiar with the statewide efforts to increase student achievement in history.

Although the Theme of the sentence is a personal pronoun, *I*, the Rheme tells the reader who Luciana will be working with for her project. From here, Luciana can then move on to describe each participant in more detail. As interviews were one of her primary data collection methods, she also includes this in Text 10.22, making it part of the hyper-Theme of the phase as well.

In the fifth phase, Data Analysis, the student researcher presents the ways in which they intend to analyze the data that they will collect. Often, they provide a sample analysis (sometimes as an Appendix) where they show how the data will be analyzed. This phase can be signaled in a rather straightforward manner, as can be seen in Text 10.23.

Text 10.23

Phase 5	(Luciana's DP example)
Data Analysis (extract only)	Data analysis will be simultaneous with data collection to maintain and sharpen the research focus, to prevent repetition, and to keep control of the database (Merriam, 1998).

Here, Luciana uses *data analysis* as her point of departure for the phase, signaling the shift from a description of her participants to one of the analysis of the previously discussed data.

The two phases, Data Analysis Table and Timeline, are both made up of tables composed of language. Thus, they are quite different from the other phases in the rest of the DP. It should be noted that we did not analyze these for thematic development as we did with other phases. However, they are still important for the DP in general and will be discussed briefly. The purpose of the Data Analysis Table (see Table 10.4) is for the writer to condense all of the information from previous stages into a coherent table. This allows the reader to step back and get a big picture view of the research being proposed. This table contains information organized into three columns labeled Research Question, Data to be Analyzed, and Anticipated Outcomes. Again, the purpose of this table is not to present new information but to condense the information already given in the DP.

Table 10.4. Data Analysis Table

Research Question	Data to be Analyzed	Anticipated Outcomes
(1) How is writing taught and understood by both teachers and students?	Interviews with principals of Riverview High Interview with Superintendent of Riverview School District	Description of administrative goals of writing instruction at Riverview High School

The final phase, Timeline, in the Methods stage is an overview of the expected time to complete the research process, including details for what part of the process will be completed and when. In Text 10.25, we see the timeline from Josh's DP where each step in the research process is given along with the season in which the research will be completed. Like the Data Analysis Table, this table serves to give condensed information for the reader to know if this timeline is actually achievable in the time presented.

Text 10.25

Phase 7	(Josh's DP example)
Timeline	• Fall 2011 to Spring 2012—data collection and on-going data analysis • Summer 2012—more in-depth data analysis • Fall 2012 to Spring 2013—writing of research report • Spring 2013—completion of dissertation

The Significance and Implications stage

The overall goal of the fourth stage, Significance and Implications, is to demonstrate the potential importance of the dissertation research to the reader. Thus, the DP writer is expected to highlight how the dissertation study will contribute to the field of her/his profession and to explain how the potential outcomes of the dissertation study might be used for pedagogical purposes in the future.

Signaling the phase. As we saw with the primary stages of the DPs above, there are general ways in which writers signal the different phases within each stage. In this section, we will name each phase within this stage of the dissertation proposal, providing a description and suggestions for how one might organize their own Significance and Implications stage. This stage has two identifiable phases as seen below in Table 10.5.

Table 10.5. The two phases of the Significance and Implications stage

Phase Number	Title of Phase
1	Potential Significance of the Study
2	Potential Implications of the Study

The Potential Significance of the Study phase functions to demonstrate the significance a dissertation study may have within the particular professional field. As we can see in the example from Luciana's DP (Text 10.26), she begins the paragraph with what is little known about the expectations for students' writing in history classes and language resources students use when they write to demonstrate their historical knowledge.

Text 10.26

Phase 1	(Luciana's DP example)
Potential Significance (extract only)	Little is known about the expectations for students' writing in history classes and language resources students use when they write to demonstrate their historical knowledge. Bringing these areas together in a research project will enable us to gain insights into a more complete view of historical literacy. This project will inform professional development leaders of student language needs and teachers' expectations for what students should be achieving in school history writing ...

The Theme is juxtaposed with the Theme in the following sentence "Bringing these areas together in a research project," signaling to readers the possible significance her dissertation study may have within the particular professional field—historical literacy. Followed by the Theme in the next sentence, *This project*, Luciana continues elaborating on the possible significance her dissertation study may contribute.

Phase 2 of the Significance and Implication Stage, the Potential Implications of the Study, is illustrated as Luciana explains how the potential outcomes of her dissertation study will contribute to the field of historical literacy and, therefore, will have implications for educational practice (i.e., school history writing; see Text 10.27). Beginning with the Theme, *Wineburg (2001) also*, Luciana cites this scholar in support of the multidisciplinary approach to explore historical understanding. The Theme is then followed by the Theme in the next sentence, *This study*, showing that her dissertation study will also draw on the multidisciplinary approach to display her participants' historical understanding. Such thematic development can lead readers to see the potential outcomes of her dissertation study and the potential implications for educational practice of teaching and learning school history.

Text 10.27

Phase 2	(Luciana's DP example)
Potential Implication of Study for Educational Practice (extract only)	Wineburg (2001) also claims, "At its heart, historical understanding is an interdisciplinary enterprise, and nothing less than a multidisciplinary approach will approximate its complexity (p. 52)." This study is going to do just that, use multidisciplinary tools, from linguistics to education, to understand historical understanding and its display in writing. In order to accomplish the goals of higher student achievement in history, we need to understand the language resources students need to control to be successful. It is only when we have a more complete picture of what knowledge and skills history students need that we will be able to accomplish our goals of providing students with opportunities to succeed in school history.

Discussion and conclusions

When embarking on their own task of proposing their dissertation research, both Josh and Shu-Wen found many useful resources which aided in the writing process and understanding of the key rhetorical elements of our own DPs. However, they also had great difficulty finding adequate linguistic descriptions of the product they were being asked to produce. By utilizing Luciana's DP as a model, they became increasingly aware of the importance of thematic development for DPs. However, aside from clear titles for each chapter and stage of the DP, there were little explicit clues as to how each phase developed within each stage. Thus, they aimed to understand the DP linguistically and not just rhetorically, as these two aspects of writing any piece are intimately connected. Understanding the way that Themes were used in Luciana's model helped them connect their own rhetorical moves to explicit linguistic choices they were making in composing their own DPs. Although we have described here a very specific kind of DP for a very specific discipline, this chapter provides a more explicit linguistic understanding of how DPs are developed thematically. With proper models to examine before writing, other DP writers should be able to know more explicitly how their linguistic choices help develop the DP as a rhetorical product.

References

Belcher, W. L. (2009). *Writing your journal article in 12 weeks: A guide to academic publishing success*. Thousand Oaks, CA: SAGE.

Glatthorn, A. (1998). *Writing the winning dissertation: A step-by-step guide*. Thousand Oaks, CA: Corwin.

Halliday, M. A. K., & Matthiessen, C. M. I. M. (2004). *An introduction to functional grammar* (3rd ed.). London: Arnold.

Kilbourn, B. (2006). The qualitative doctoral dissertation. *Teachers College Record*, *108*(4), 529–576.

Krathwohl, D., & Smith, N. (2005). *How to prepare a dissertation proposal: Suggestions for students in education and behavioral sciences*. Syracuse, NY: Syracuse University Press.

Macken-Horarik, M. (2002). "Something to shoot for": A systemic functional approach to teaching genre in secondary school science. In A. M. Johns (Ed.), *Genre in the classroom: Multiple perspectives* (pp. 17–42). Mahwah, NJ: Erlbaum.

Martin, J. R., & Rose, D. (2008). *Genre relations: Mapping culture*. London: Equinox.

Meloy, J. (2001). *Writing the qualitative dissertation: Understanding by doing*. Mahwah, NJ: Erlbaum.

Silva, P. (2007). *How to write a lot: A practical guide to productive academic writing*. Washington, DC: American Psychological Association.

Index

www.ingramcontent.com/pod-product-compliance
Lightning Source LLC
LaVergne TN
LVHW010348080826
844660LV00003B/220
* 9 7 8 1 8 4 5 5 3 2 4 1 3 *